THE CATHOLIC UNIVERSITY OF AMERICA
CANON LAW STUDIES
Number 55

THE PRINCIPLES OF DELEGATION

A DISSERTATION

SUBMITTED TO THE FACULTY OF CANON LAW OF THE CATHOLIC UNIVERSITY OF AMERICA IN PARTIAL FULFILLMENT OF THE REQUIREMENTS FOR THE DEGREE OF

DOCTOR OF CANON LAW

BY

RAYMOND A. KEARNEY, A.B., S.T.D., J.C.L.
Priest of the Diocese of Brooklyn

THE CATHOLIC UNIVERSITY OF AMERICA
WASHINGTON, D. C.
1929

Nihil Obstat:

IACOBUS HUGO RYAN, Ph.D., S.T.D.,
Rector Magnificus Universitatis,
Censor Deputatus.
Washingtonii, D. C., die XXI Maii, 1929.

Imprimatur:

✠THOMAS EDMUNDUS MOLLOY, D.D.,
Episcopus Brooklyniensis.
Brooklynii, die XXXI Maii, 1929.

TABLE OF CONTENTS

Part II

Commentary

FOREWORD

The delegation of power is a most common instrument in the government of the Church. Delegation, in its fundamental notion, is merely the accomplishing through the services of another what one is empowered to do himself. The great volume of ecclesiastical affairs that occupy the time and attention of the Superiors of the Church, demands the possibility of entrusting much to the care of subordinates. Thus, delegation contributes much to the efficiency of ecclesiastical administration and government.

The present dissertation does not essay to enter into the varied fields of law in which the delegation of power regularly finds its place. To do this is obviously impossible in a work of this type. Hence, general principles, and not specific applications, constitute the matter of this volume. The first part is an historical study, in which the existence and development of the principles throughout ecclesiastical history are briefly indicated. The second part deals with the principles of delegation as they are contained in the new law of the Code.

The writer takes this occasion to express his gratitude to the Right Reverend Monsignor Filippo Bernardini, S.T.D., J.U.D., Dean of the School of Canon Law, for his generous assistance in the preparation of this dissertation. He also acknowledges his indebtedness to the Reverend Valentine Schaaf, O.F.M., J.C.D., the Reverend Hubert L. Motry, S.T.D., J.C.D., and the Reverend Francis J. Lardone, S.T.D., J.U.D., all of the Faculty of the School of Canon Law of the Catholic University of America, for invaluable suggestions and guidance.

PART I—HISTORICAL STUDY

CHAPTER I

Earliest Evidences of Delegation

The concept of delegation is a simple one. The jurists have expressed it in various legal axioms that are in themselves patent. The *Regulae Iuris* of Boniface VIII present the fundamental notion of delegation when they state: *Qui facit per alium, est perinde, ac si faciat per seipsum;* [1] and again: *Potest quis per alium, quod potest facere per seipsum.*[2] This notion is natural, not artificial; the most elementary reasoning suggests its accuracy. It is a proximate deduction of the very law of nature, and its first origin antedates the codification of all law.

Jethro [3] found Moses, his kinsman, wearied and spent, because from morning till night the great Law-giver had been judging the controversies of his people. Jethro gave this counsel:

> Provide out of all the people able men, such as fear God . . . who may judge the people at all times: and when any great matter soever shall fall out, let them refer it to thee, and let them judge the lesser matters only: that so it may be lighter for thee, the burden being shared out unto others.

Moses heeded this counsel. This is the first delegation of power that Sacred Scripture narrates.

The present volume cannot undertake the task of outlining the story of delegation throughout the course of human history. It is possible merely to indicate the existence of this legal instrument during the various periods of the Christian era. The first evidences may be found in the very beginning of Christianity.

1 Reg. 72, R. J., in VI.
2 Reg. 68, R. J., in VI.
3 Exodus, XVIII.

Hence, the present chapter will consider the existence of delegation as found in ecclesiastical and civil documents of the first centuries—Sacred Scripture and Roman law.

Article I.—Delegation in Sacred Scripture

The Apostles heeded the command of Christ to go forth and to teach all nations. They hastened about, preaching, baptizing and laying the foundations of the prospective Christian communities. Whenever it was possible, they ruled and governed the churches by their personal contact and influence. When, however, this direct, personal action was not possible, these pioneers of Christianity did not, therefore, forfeit the government of the churches. From afar they ruled the churches of their conception, and the Pastoral Epistles give ample testimony of this fact. Paul did not write mere moral exhortations to his absent brethren, but he wrote as one having authority. To the Corinthians he wrote, "Therefore I write these things, being absent, that, being present, I may not deal more severely, according to the power which the Lord hath given me unto edification and not unto destruction." [4] Again he asked them, "What will you? Shall I come to you with a rod, or in charity, and in the spirit of meekness?" [5] The reference to the rod is obviously a suggestion that he would use stern authority, if need be. Again, concerning the adulterer he wrote, "I indeed, absent in body, but present in spirit, have already judged, as though I were present, him that hath so done." [6] The Apostle then pronounced the sentence of excommunication, an act clearly enough reserved to one in authority. Examples might be multiplied, were it necessary, to indicate the high jurisdiction that the Apostle enjoyed over the churches he had founded. As long as he lived, Paul was indeed the Pastor of his flocks.[7]

The Apostle accomplished much by personal contact with the Christian communities; in periods of absence his letters made known to the churches that their spiritual father was yet solicitous for their intensive and extensive development. This,

---

[4] 2 Cor., XIII, 10.
[5] 1 Cor., IV, 21.
[6] 1 Cor., V, 3.
[7] Ruffini, *Introductio in Novum Testamentum,* II, 260.

however, did not suffice. The epistles were few comparatively, and Paul was rarely present for a considerable time in any one church. The local government of the churches was in the hands of the presbyters or elders, who exercised authority as a collegiate body.[8] The Apostle was reluctant to leave such a group, composed of recent converts whose minds had yet to be purged of innate prejudices, superstitions and worldly ambitions, entirely on its own resources. He was frequently suspicious of the elders and often exhorted them against ministering for gain.[9] To combat such difficulty Paul found it necessary to place in a position of prudent authority men more deeply imbued with solid Christian mind and character. It is with genuine pride that Paul can refer to Timothy in this manner, "I have no man so of the same mind, who with sincere affection is solicitous for you." [10] It is Timothy's sympathetic spirit that makes him above all commendable. By the aid of this associate and other distinguished men of kindred spirit Paul kept watch over the first-born flocks of his Master. It is in these eminent cooperators of Paul in the sacred ministry that the first Christian evidences of delegation may be discovered. They labored in the name of Paul and by virtue of authority committed to them by the Apostle, and not by virtue of any authority that can be conceived as properly their own.

Paul wrote to Titus, "For this cause I left thee in Crete that thou shouldst set in order the things that are wanting and shouldst ordain priests in every city, as I also appointed thee." [11] Now Crete was not a city, but a great island, densely populated, and composed of many distinct communities.[12] Crete was therefore a great ecclesiastical province, including many distinct churches, which constituted as many localized ecclesiastical units. Consequently, the duty of Titus was not that of a diocesan bishop, who presides over one canonical unit, but his task was to set in order the affairs of every church and to ordain

[8] Moran, *The Government of the Church in the First Century,* p. 181; Ruffini, *op. cit.,* II, 265.

[9] Moran, *op. cit.,* p. 176.

[10] Phil., II, 20.

[11] Tit., I, 5.

[12] Cornelius a Lapide, *Commentaria in Omnes D. Pauli Epistolas,* p. 857. This author states that the Poet wrote of Crete, "Urbes centum habitat magnas, ditissima regna."

presbyters in every city. He exercised therefore an authority that was wider than diocesan and superior to it.

Wernz,[13] while he does not discuss at length the possibility that Titus was a delegate of the Apostle, suggests it at least in passing. In general, however, older authors have regarded Titus as enjoying an office in Crete identical with, or very similar to, the present archiepiscopacy.[14] This latter opinion does not seem well sustained. It is not at all clear that the hierarchy of the church had been developed to such a degree of perfection during the lives of the Apostles. Cornelius a Lapide writes, "It is plain that Christ did not arrange all things, but He left much to the Apostles and their successors concerning the government of the church, to be arranged according to the needs of the future. The prudent institution of any state demands this."[15] It is a matter of faith that by divine disposition the hierarchy is composed of bishops, priests and ministers.[16] Moreover, it is true that from the very beginning the hierarchy existed perfect in these three essential degrees.[17] The archbishopric, however, is not an essential, but makes for greater unity and solidarity. The existence of this office is not necessarily conceived at the beginning, since the Apostles themselves directed the many churches they had founded and thus naturally existed as the bonds of unity between the communities. It is only because of the fact that the apostolic age was of its nature unusual and the power of the Apostles extraordinary,[18] that it became in the course of time necessary to create an office of the nature of the archbishopric. Badii notes that in Timothy and Titus *obscure indications* of the power of metropolitans may be found; and he further notes that only in the course of time was this jurisdiction evolved and well defined.[19]

That the duty of Titus did not correspond precisely with the present notion of the archbishopric is further made clear from the fact that Titus did not enjoy at Crete a permanent office.

---

[13] II, n. 551, not. 13.

[14] Cornelius a Lapide, *op. cit.*, p. 853; Bernardinus a Piconio, *Epistolarum B. Pauli Apostoli Triplex Expositio,* III, 190.

[15] *Op. cit.*, p. 857.

[16] Council of Trent, sess. XXIII, *de ordine,* can. 6.

[17] Ruffini, *op. cit.*, II, 259.

[18] Phillips, *Compendium Juris Ecclesiastici,* p. 102.

[19] *Institutiones Juris Canonici,* n. 202.

Had he been the incumbent of a permanent ecclesiastical office, his jurisdiction, deriving from that office, would necessarily be regarded as ordinary, and not delegated.[20] The Sacred Scriptures, however, seem to indicate that Titus was not a permanent official of the church of Crete.

Paul wrote, "When I shall send to thee Artemas or Tychicus, make haste to come to me to Nicopolis." [21] In the second epistle to Timothy, written after the epistle to Titus, it is stated that Luke alone remains with Paul, for Titus has gone to Dalmatia. It is to be noted that the recall of Titus from Crete does not occasion an explanation from Paul; the command is peremptory. Moran writes, "It is not the tearing away of a bishop from his flock, but the recall of a legate, who had been sent on a special temporary mission. Titus holds in the spiritual province a position like that of the proconsul in the civil; he is a pro-apostle, exercising by delegation the supreme control over the Christian municipalities." [22] Paul would not have recalled Titus so peremptorily, if such a recall had been entirely unexpected; the Apostle was wont to deal with his cooperators with abundant charity and affection, and not with the promptness of a military commandant. Not only subsequently to his Cretan mission, but also before he labored there, Titus served in a similar capacity among the Corinthians. Paul writing to the Corinthians refers to Titus as "my companion and fellow labourer towards you." [23] That Titus exercised there a real authority cannot be denied, for Paul commended the Corinthians precisely because they had obeyed, "remembering the obedience of you all, how with fear and trembling you received him." [24] It is therefore probable that Titus ministered unto many other churches during his lengthy association with Paul, whose confidence and affection he fully enjoyed.[25] The temporary capacity in which Titus served in the Pauline churches, indicates with a certain degree of probability that Titus was a pro-apostle, the delegate of Paul.

---

[20] Wernz-Vidal, *Jus Canonicum,* II, n. 518.

[21] Tit., III, 12.

[22] *Op. cit.,* p. 164.

[23] 2 Cor., VIII, 23.

[24] 2 Cor., VII, 15.

[25] MacEvilly, *An Exposition of the Epistles of St. Paul and of the Catholic Epistles,* II, 140.

What has been said of Titus, may be repeated with some security of Timothy, who is the outstanding figure in the edification of the church of Ephesus, the metropolis of pro-consular Asia. There was no one so dear to Paul as Timothy; [26] and the Apostle employed this fervent bishop for many missionary activities.

Timothy served in a temporary capacity among the Thessalonians, to whom Paul wrote, "And we sent Timothy, our brother, and the minister of God in the Gospel of Christ, to confirm you and exhort you concerning your faith." [27] In the same context Paul recalls the return of Timothy from Thessalonica and the joy attendant thereon, since Timothy bore testimony of the faith and charity of that people.[28] Corinth too was a field wherein Timothy toiled, and in his letter to the Corinthians Paul makes clear that he has sent Timothy precisely because he himself is unable to come. Timothy will remind them of Paul; [29] he will be the representative, the *alter ego* of the Apostle.

When Timothy presided at Ephesus, Paul still retained the rule of that community. From afar he directed the activities of his assistant. He said to Timothy, "These things I write to thee, hoping that I shall come to thee shortly. But if I tarry long, that thou mayest know how thou oughtest to behave thyself in the house of God which is the church of the living God." [30] Finally when the Apostle sensed the approach of death, he summoned Timothy away from his people, "Make haste to come to me quickly. . . . Make haste to come before winter." [31] The recall of Timothy, like that of Titus, occasioned the nomination of a substitute, and Tychicus had already been dispatched to Ephesus, when Timothy was recalled.[32]

The opinion that Timothy was a delegate of Paul is confirmed from other sources. Bernardinus a Piconio states that Paul frequently sent Timothy where he himself could not go, and

---

[26] McGiffert, *The Apostolic Age,* p. 428.
[27] 1 Thess., III, 2.
[28] 1 Thess., III, 6.
[29] 1 Cor., IV, 17.
[30] 1 Tim., III, 14.
[31] 2 Tim., IV, 9 sq.
[32] 2 Tim., IV, 12.

indeed in the role of *legatus a latere.*[33] Joannes a Gorcum writes that the Apostle deemed it necessary frequently to admonish Timothy and Titus in his epistles to them, although he had instructed them abundantly, when he first *delegated* to them the care of the churches.[34] More forceful still is a testimony of the fifth century, coming as it does from the lips of the Supreme Pontiff. Innocent I sent Rufus as his delegate to Thessalonica, and in so doing he proclaimed that he acted in imitation of Paul, who delegated to Titus and Timothy the care of the churches of Crete and Asia respectively.[35]

The opinion just exposed cannot be regarded as more than a probability. It is difficult to ascertain precisely the functions of ecclesiastics of this period; documents are rare and the Scriptures afford only some light on this matter. It is even more difficult to determine the nature of the jurisdiction wielded by the coaevals of the Apostles. Many writers have long regarded them as the ordinary officers of their respective churches. To these writers, however, traces of delegation in Sacred Scripture must remain evident; for if Titus was the ordinary standard-bearer at Crete, then surely Artemas or Tychicus, whom Paul sent to relieve Titus whilst the latter should be journeying to Nicopolis, was a delegate, who would supply the absence of Titus, as commentators generally assert.[36] The same may be said in the case of Timothy, whose absence from Ephesus more clearly, perhaps, was but temporary. Tychicus supplied the place of Timothy, who hastened to Rome to be with the Apostle before the latter should be executed.[37] Again, the commentators, who have regarded Timothy as the ordinary superior of Ephesus, look upon Tychicus as a substitute, deriving authority from Paul, and designated merely in a temporary capacity until such a time as Timothy should be free to return.[38]

The opinion set forth in these pages may be extended to all,

[33] *Op. cit.*, III, 12.

[34] Migne, *Sacrae Scripturae Cursus Completus,* XXV, 177.

[35] Mansi, VIII, 751.

[36] Van Steenkiste, *S. Pauli Epistolae Breviter Explicatae,* II, 439; Joannes a Gorcum, *op. cit.*, Migne, XXV, 213; Cornelius a Lapide, *op. cit.*, p. 873; Bernardinus a Piconio, *op. cit.*, III, 213.

[37] 2 Tim., IV, 12.

[38] Bernardinus a Piconio, *op. cit.*, III, 177; Van Steenkiste, *op. cit.*, II, 398; MacEvilly, *op. cit.*, II, 138.

or most of, the communities, which Paul had evangelized, since in all of these he very likely maintained an identical system of government.[39] Paul remained until death the Apostle of all the Gentiles,[40] and his legates carried on the ministry in the name, spirit, and authority of their leader.

Article II.—Roman Law

Roman law has left to posterity a wealth of splendid juristic principles. In no field, perhaps, has it left so great an impression as in the canon law of all ages. In the matter with which this work is concerned Roman law has left more than a mere influence; it is the very basis and foundation of the legislation regarding the delegation of power. The Code has incorporated many principles of Roman law directly into the current legislation of the Church. Many other principles have been added that custom or practice have made sacred. A clear conception of the Roman legislation on matters of delegation will be a considerable aid in the interpretation of subsequent legislation on the same subject.

§*1*. *Delegation in Roman Law*

In Roman law the term delegation has enjoyed a meaning far wider than the same term bears in modern law. Delegation naturally implies a substitution of persons. Modern law has restricted the sense of the term to a substitution of persons in the exercise of jurisdiction or of some power that may be likened to jurisdiction. In addition to this meaning, delegation in Roman law had another distinctly technical signification, implying the substitution of persons with regard to obligations. Thus the Digests state: "To delegate is to give to a creditor another debtor in one's stead." [41] From this text Buckland has formulated a concise definition of delegation, calling it *substitution of a debtor's debtor*.[42] Thus if A was indebted to B to

[39] Moran, *op. cit.*, p. 172.

[40] St. Thomas Aquinas, *Commentaria in Omnes D. Pauli Apostoli Epistolas*, III, 151.

[41] Fr. 11, D. 46, 2; fr. 6, D. 16, 1; fr. 9, D. 19, 5; cf. Prateio, *Lexicon Juris*, V. *Delegatio*.

[42] *A Manual of Roman Private Law*, p. 566.

the extent of ten; and C was indebted to A to the same extent; by force of delegation C would become indebted directly to B and no further relation would exist between A and B, in so far as this particular transaction is concerned. C, the debtor of A, would have been substituted as the debtor of B; and instead of two distinct debts, one alone would exist after the process had been completed.

It is to be noted that the text just quoted, refers to creditors and debtors. These terms, too, in Roman law had a wider extension than is given to them in the modern systems. Thus, in Roman law the debtor was a person who had an obligation of any description whatsoever towards another, while the creditor was the person who enjoyed the right corresponding to this obligation.[43] The same terms, at least in English law, are now restricted exclusively to the persons involved in a monetary transaction.[44]

The effect of delegation was primarily the extinction of an obligation on the part of a debtor, when the creditor of the latter accepted a new debtor in his place.[45] Indeed, the effect was so absolute that even if later the delegated debtor should not be equal to the payment of his debt, the creditor could exercise no claim on the first debtor, once the transaction had been perfected.[46] Since the creditor's rights might be jeopardized by an unfavorable substitution, no such delegation could be effected without the consent of the creditor.[47]

The meaning of delegation, as just exposed, has been limited to the case where a creditor has substituted in his stead one who is indebted to him to the same extent as he in turn is indebted to a third party. This was the strict meaning of the term. Delegation, however, was used in a broader sense, and not quite properly, whenever a person promised to pay the debt of another, although he who so promised was in no way obliged to do so.[48] Thus, if one out of mere friendship would offer to undergo the indebtedness of a colleague, and the substitution

[43] Dig. 50, 16, 11; dig. 60, 16, 108.

[44] Sherman, *Roman Law in the Modern World,* II, 291.

[45] Cod. 8, 41, 3; dig. 46, 2, 12.

[46] Gaj. 3, 176; Just. Inst. 3, 29, 3.

[47] Cod. 8, 41, 1.

[48] Buckland, *A Text-Book of Roman Law,* p. 566.

would have been agreed to, this would be a case of delegation in a less proper sense.

Poste [49] has concluded that delegation in the sense exposed was a frequently used instrument in the commercial transactions of the Romans, and he cites as an example the fact that the father of Cicero supplied his son with money, when the latter was a student at Athens, by the mediation of a certain Atticus who had debtors in Greece.

The use of the term delegation with regard to the substitution of persons in the payment of debts is nowhere to be found in the present legislation of the Church. This, however, does not signify that the expression was unknown in earlier ecclesiastical legislation. The collections of decisions of the Rota reveal a few cases in which the term was recognized and used in similar negotiations in the ecclesiastical forum.[50]

The use of delegation in Roman law as applied to commercial transactions was not exclusive. It enjoyed also a meaning that has had more influence on modern law than the use just presented. Delegation in modern law has come to mean the substitution of persons in the exercise of authority or power. This sense of the term had a prominent place in Roman law.

In the first place, the sources of Roman law contain frequent reference to *potestas mandata*. This mandated power substantially is the same as delegation, although some differences may be indicated. He who has delegated power, possesses the power of another, and not what may properly be conceived as his own; the delegate acts in the name of him who has commissioned him, and by virtue of the commissioner's authority. This same concept is found verified in its essentials in the mandated power of Roman law. Thus Ulpian in the Digests wrote that the Praetor is wont to commit his jurisdiction either totally or partially; he to whom it is thus committed, fulfills not his own office but the office of him who has delegated him.[51] And Papinian said, "He who has assumed mandated jurisdiction, has nothing properly his own, but he uses the power of the person who has committed it." [52] These texts reveal, therefore, the identity of

---

[49] *Gai Institutiones Iuris Civilis*, p. 382.
[50] *Decisiones Nuperrimae*, vol. III, dec. 169, n. 16.
[51] Fr. 16, D. 2, 1.
[52] Fr. 1, D. 1, 21.

concept of both delegated and mandated power. The mandated power, as well as delegation, is not attached to an office, but belongs to another, in whose name and right it is exercised. Where Roman law refers to mandated power, it is reasonable to conclude that the term delegation, with slight variations, may be substituted.

More than this, Roman law also clearly makes use of the term delegation, particularly where the sources refer to judges and tribunals. Thus, Justinian speaks clearly of delegated judges when he distinguishes between those situated in the magistracies, those appointed by the royal court and those delegated by inferiors.[53] The same jurist also refers to them as those "to whom we have committed a hearing or those who are designated by the higher judges." [54] Again, where the sources impose restrictions within which the delegation of power must be contained, it is written, "A judge delegated by another judge cannot *give a judge* unless he was appointed by the emperor." [55] The Digests distinguish between those things which a magistrate enjoys by virtue of his office and those attributed to him in a special manner by a law, decree or constitution. They assert that the former may be delegated, but not the latter, and, hence, that those magistrates who, enjoying a delegated jurisdiction, commit it to another, are in error.[56] In this text the jurist evidently admits the principle of delegation, but within definitely circumscribed limits. Justinian in the Novels imposed on his magistrates an obligation of using definitely appointed judges in the event that they would desire to delegate particular cases.[57]

It must be remembered that judicial actions in Roman law of the very nature of the Roman judicial system gave occasion to most frequent delegations. Until a late date Roman process was divided into two distinct stages, namely, *in iure*, and *in iudicio*. Thus, in the period in which the *Legis Actio* was the normal form of procedure, the litigants appeared before the magistrate

[53] "Sive in magistratibus positi, vel ex aula nostra dati, vel a nostris proceribus delegati,"—Cod. 3, 1, 13.

[54] Cod. 3, 1, 14.

[55] "Iudicem dare; . . . nisi a principe iudex datus fuerit,"—Cod. 3, 1, 5.

[56] Fr. 1, D. 1, 21.

[57] Nov. 82, 2, 2.

and by use of certain invariable phrases presented their difficulty; the action was then *in iure*. By order of the magistrate the action was then referred to a judge who reviewed the case and decided on the merits of the question; the case was then said to be *in iudicio*. The judges were in this process selected by the parties or by the magistrate from the *album iudicum*, or list of reputable citizens, in much the same manner as jurors are selected in modern law.

The *Formulary System* succeeded the *Legis Actio*. This new system took much of the stiffness out of the previous procedure. "The magistrate," writes Buckland,[58] "was no longer an automaton, reciting words prescribed for him; he controlled the proceedings." His power increased and he tempered justice with common sense. The review of the facts, however, and the decision were still entrusted to a judge. The same two stages, *in iure*, and *in iudicio*, were preserved.[59] The Praetor committed the case to a judge of his choosing and approved antecedently the decision that would be rendered.[60]

Another judicial system was the *Cognitio Extraordinaria*, in which the distinction of two stages disappeared. The magistrate, or his delegate, before whom the case was first introduced, heard and decided the entire affair.[61] Diocletian (A. D. 294) forbade the governors of the provinces to delegate cases to judges, except when the pressure of business demanded such assistance.[62]

A word must be added about the *iudices pedanei*, who sat in the *subsellia*, as if at the feet of the Praetor, from which fact they derived their name.[63] It was to these that the governors had been wont to commit cases before the enactment of Diocletian.[64] Sherman [65] calls them "permanent petty judges." Their original function is described by Julian in these words: "There are certain matters for which it is unnecessary to await

[58] *A Text-Book of Roman Law*, p. 603.

[59] Buckland, *A Manual of Roman Private Law*, p. 360; Poste, *Gai Institutiones Iuris Civilis*, p. 474.

[60] Radin, *Handbook of Roman Law*, p. 27.

[61] Buckland, *A Text-Book of Roman Law*, p. 604.

[62] Cod. 3, 3, 2.

[63] "Ad pedes"; cf. Adam, *Roman Antiquities*, p. 165.

[64] Buckland, *A Text-Book of Roman Law*, p. 659; Leage, *Roman Private Law*, p. 380; Roberti, *De Processibus*, I, n. 146.

[65] *Roman Law in the Modern World*, II, n. 901.

the moderator of the province; therefore, we concede to the governors the faculty of naming petty judges, that is, those who may hear the less serious cases."[66] They were, therefore, a type of delegated judges who after Diocletian were not to be employed except under extraordinary circumstances and only in the more simple matters that came up for decision.[67]

An important principle of modern legislation has also its foundation in Roman law. Thus it is read: "To whomsoever is entrusted jurisdiction, those things also seem to be conceded without which that jurisdiction could not be exercised."[68] And Paul in the Digests writes: "If jurisdiction is committed to a private person, authority too seems to be committed, for jurisdiction without moderate coaction is useless."[69] Thus it was that when the magistrate committed a case *in iudicio* to a private individual, this person was the recipient of whatever authority or *imperium* needed for the felicitous execution of his duty.[70]

§2. *Subdelegation in Roman Law*

Subdelegation is mediate delegation; it proceeds, not from one who has power in his own right, but from one who is himself a delegate. The delegation of power must naturally be contained within certain well defined limits. Subdelegation in modern ecclesiastical law is permitted under certain conditions. Was it an acknowledged method in Roman law? Recently, one writer[71] has come to the conclusion that there is no solid foundation to assert the existence of subdelegation in Roman law. This opinion is based on a few citations from the sources. Thus, the Digests state, "It is manifest that no one can commit to another jurisdiction already committed to himself."[72] And again, "He can commit jurisdiction who enjoys it in his own right and not by virtue of another's benevolence."[73] These

[66] Cod. 3, 3, 5.
[67] Declareuil, *Rome the Law-Giver*, p. 322.
[68] Fr. 2, D. 2, 1.
[69] Fr. 5, D. 1, 21.
[70] Radin, *Handbook of Roman Law*, p. 37; Morey, *Outlines of Roman Law*, p. 388.
[71] "De Potestate Delegata ad Universitatem Causarum deque ejus Subdelegabilitate," *Jus Pont.*, VIII (1928), 183-198.
[72] Fr. 5, D. 1, 21.
[73] Fr. 5, D. 2, 1.

texts are quite clear and have caused the greater part of commentators to regard subdelegation as unknown in Roman law.[74]

There are, however, other texts[75] which indicate that the delegated judge could appoint another judge (*iudicem dare*). Whether or not the naming of such a judge (*iudicem dando*) is the same as the act of delegating a judge, is uncertain. A truly delegated judge could summon to court, hear the case and execute the sentence; whereas, the *iudex datus* was not competent to perform all the functions of the delegate.[76] Bouix,[77] however, seems to indicate the identity of subdelegation and the faculty expressed in the phrase *iudicem dare.*

Whether or not subdelegation was an institution of Roman law, remains obscure. Most of the moderns have adopted the view that subdelegation was introduced into canon law through a false interpretation of Roman law.[78]

---

[74] Maroto, *Institutiones,* I, 840, not. c.

[75] Cod. 3, 1, 5; fr. 12, D. 5, 1, etc.

[76] Roberti, *De Processibus,* I, n. 146.

[77] *De Judicis Ecclesiasticis,* I, 146: ". . . potestatem dandi iudicem, id est, subdelegandi."

[78] Maroto, *Institutiones,* I, 840, not. c; cf. *Jus. Pont.,* VIII (1928), 184.

CHAPTER II

The History of Delegation from the First to the Sixth Century

Church law, in so far as it is positive and human, adapted itself considerably to the civil law that was recognized in the early centuries of the Christian era. Since civil law, and in a preeminent way, Roman law, made no attempt to treat scientifically of general and abstract principles, but rather applied principles as occasion demanded, so too canon law from the beginning was not a systematized body of truths or principles. Consequently, a study of a particular canonical institution, such as delegation, must lead into a wide field of historical research, if general principles are to be extracted from their connatural surroundings.

Article I.—Papal Delegation

A history of the institution which is here to be treated, will not be found in well formulated juridical principles; it must be gleaned from facts which will demonstrate that delegation has been a legal instrument of long standing, and which will, at the same time, manifest the evolution of this institution. Literary monuments of the first centuries naturally speak more frequently of the Roman Pontiff than of his inferiors. Hence, the early history of delegation will be found in a particular manner centered about the many delegates or legates whom the Popes saw fit to dispatch to distant places whither they themselves were either unable or unwilling to go, for the purpose of expediting important ecclesiastical affairs. In later periods much light is cast upon this institute by the vast legislation that treats of delegated judges and tribunals. These two classes, therefore, will constitute the sources of the information that will be proposed in the following pages.

§*1. Legates of the Holy See*

Pope Pius VI has gathered into one volume[1] a wealth of information that regards the legates who went forth from the Apostolic See, armed with the authority of the Supreme Head of the Christian Church. This work was occasioned by the attack of four Metropolitans who had been affected by the taint of heresy. These German bishops, by opposing the right of the Supreme Pontiff to send representatives equipped with jurisdictional authority into all parts of the Christian world, in reality denied the true concept of the primacy of Rome. It was in respect to this denial that Pius VI wrote:

> It is question of a serious and a signal right of the Primacy instituted in Peter and his successors by Christ. The Roman Pontiff, endowed with this right, whilst he bears the universal care of the lambs and sheep entrusted to him, exercises his apostolic office by means of ecclesiastical men, either permanently established, or delegated for a time, as he might deem more expedient, in those distant places where he cannot intervene, instructing them to supply there his place and to exercise that authority, which he himself would wield, were he present.[2]

In asserting the right of the Holy See to send legates abroad Pius has distinguished between those who perform a permanent duty of representing the Holy See, and those who only for a period of time engage in this honorable task.[3] Those who have represented the Pope by virtue of a temporary commission to discharge one or a few definite and specific matters, and who were therefore equipped with some measure of jurisdiction, are of prime importance in the present duty. These obviously have labored by virtue of a delegation of authority, since to them has been assigned no stable or permanent ecclesiastical function, without which ordinary jurisdiction, in so far as it is opposed to delegated jurisdiction, cannot be conceived.

The agents of the Holy See who have enjoyed an office to which a certain permanency had been attached, are not to be

---

[1] *Responsio ad Metropolitanos Moguntinum, Trevirensem, Coloniensem, Salisburgensem, super Nuntiaturis Apostolicis,* Romae, 1789.

[2] *Op. cit.*, p. 170.

[3] "Per ecclesiasticos viros, sive stabiles, sive ad tempus, veluti magis expedire censuerit, delegatos . . ."—*ibid.*

disregarded altogether. It is not at all certain that even these enjoyed power that may be considered ordinary according to the notions of the nature of jurisdiction prevailing before the Code. The value of the permanent legations of the Holy See will be discussed more opportunely, when the history of the permanent Vicariate of Thessalonica will be presented for consideration. It is sufficient for the present to remark that even these permanently established legations can be of material assistance in formulating the historical study, especially in the earliest periods of church history.

§2. *Adversaries*

No one denies the fundamental concept of delegation, which is merely the execution of an act through the instrumentality of another. An action performed by an individual, and an action effected by another in the name of the same individual, is morally identical. Hence the fundamental principle of delegation is unassailable.

It is one thing to admit the principle; it is another to admit the fact. History reveals a group of adversaries who have denied the fact of the exercise of Papal delegation by legates of the Holy See in regions beyond the immediate local jurisdiction of the Bishop of Rome. These opponents do not deny the fact because they would quarrel with the principles of delegation involved therein; but they do so because of their unorthodox concept of the Primacy. Condemning the jurisdictional Primacy of the Pope, they have denied the right of the Pontiff to exercise true jurisdiction over the universal church. As a result, they have logically denied too the right of the Pope to exercise jurisdiction throughout the church by means of legates or delegates whom he might dispatch to represent the Holy See in distant dioceses or provinces.

Among such opponents the four Metropolitans, against whom Pius VI directed his famous *Responsio,* are eminent. These prelates contended that the Pope could send legates only in extraordinary cases, and they insisted it was their right to determine when such urgency existed.

A conspicuous adversary arose in the person of Justin Febronius who composed a volume that directly attacked the primacy of jurisdiction enjoyed by the Roman Pontiff.[4] In this work the author rejected the concept of a monarchical form of ecclesiastical government; all the Apostles, he maintained, were equal, and to Peter was assigned nothing more than a primacy of honor, such as the president of a senate might enjoy over his fellows.[5] The genuine nature of ecclesiastical society, according to Febronius, evolved only in the course of time to the condition of a monarchy, and he has indicated at great length the causes which nurtured this unhealthy development.[6] Among these the false decretals of the pseudo-Isidore are given the primacy of importance in effecting this radical change in the constitution of the church. Febronius maintained that this colossal fraud was the sole basis for the juridical primacy of the Roman See.[7]

Febronius attempted to steer a middle course between Protestantism and the orthodox faith. He condemned the notion of the primacy as it was conceived by Wiclef, Huss, Luther and Calvin, who had reduced the primacy to a mere name; [8] and at the same time he outlined real rights that he readily conceded to the Holy See. He denied, however, the right to exercise jurisdiction over the universal church, and conceded to the Papacy only a right of universal inspection and visitation.[9]

Febronius naturally, in consequence to his opinions just exposed, denied that the Pope could exercise authority outside of Rome through the medium of legates. He contended that until the time of the false decretals no such exercise of jurisdiction had been known, and that only subsequently to the great fraud was the power of legates increased and the authority of bishops and metropolitans proportionately decreased,[10] until finally the Council of Trent applied restraints to check this rising danger.[11]

Imbued with much the same spirit as Febronius, Van Espen, a Louvain professor, fell into serious error, writing as follows:

> The delegation of jurisdiction seems to have entered the ecclesiastical forum after this forum began to be governed

[4] *De Statu Ecclesiae et Legitima Potestate Romani Pontificis,* Bullioni, 1764.

[5] *Op. cit.,* cap. II, 4, p. 83-5.

[6] *Op. cit.,* cap. III, p. 128 ss.

[7] *Op. cit.,* cap. III, 9, p. 164 ss.; cap. VIII, 1, p. 515 ss.

[8] *Op. cit.,* cap. II, 4, p. 83.

[9] *Op. cit.,* cap. II, 4, per totum.

[10] *Op. cit.,* cap. II, 10, p. 113 ss.

[11] Sess. XXIV, de ref., cap. 20.

> in the manner of the secular courts: that is, about the twelfth or thirteenth century. This is rendered more likely by the fact that neither under the title *De Rescriptis*, nor under that *De Officio et Potestate Judicis Delegati*, in the works of Gregory IX is there found a decretal more ancient than Alexander III, who died in 1181, just the time when ecclesiastical tribunals began to be directed like the secular courts.[12]

Van Espen contended that only in this late period were appeals directed to Rome for a decisive sentence in judicial matters, and that consequently then only did frequent delegation become a necessity.[13] He further saw in the permanent apostolic legations that had been erected in many important sees a vain effort of the Roman See to aggrandize power and gain prestige among the more illustrious churches.[14]

The writers here mentioned represent a school of thought, to which the Gallicans and the proponents of Josephinism readily subscribed. It was owing to the great extent of this error that Pius VI was induced to draw up an authentic refutation. The Pope was careful to avoid in his treatise the use of any facts that could not be substantiated by a more authentic source than the pseudo-Isidore; his proof is, therefore, quite independent of the principal source of what the adversaries regard as the modern false concept of the nature of ecclesiastical society.

In the pages that follow some instances will be advanced, which will indicate that the delegation of jurisdiction has been a constant practice in the church from the earliest times, and which will, at the same time, illustrate the evolution of delegation as an instrument of government.

§3. *The Presidency of the Councils*

No council can be regarded as truly ecumenical at which the chief bishop of all Christendom has not intervened. "This is so clear," writes Hefele, "that the most violent partisans of the

---

[12] Par. III, tit. V, cap. II, n. 3.

[13] Devoti thus ridicules this opinion: "Plane risum et stomachum movet quorumdam vel imperitia vel malitiosa calliditas qui apostolicos delegatos tantum saeculo XII inductos putant . . . ," *Jus Universum*, lib. I, tit. XXIX, par. 3.

[14] Par. I, tit. XXI, cap. I, n. 14.

episcopal system, who assign to the Pope only a primacy of honour (primatus honoris), yet do not in the least impugn his right to preside at ecumenical synods." [15]

The intervention of the Supreme Pontiff at a general synod may be verified in several ways. The subsequent approval of the acts of the synod by the Pope is itself an act sufficient to endow the convention with the nature of an ecumenical council, if other requisites have been verified.[16] In this manner the Fifth Ecumenical Council was approved by Pope Vigilius in his decree to Eutychius of Constantinople on December 8, 553, and later in his *Constitutum* of February 23, 554.[17] Or, as is more than evident, if the Supreme Pontiff presides in person over a universal synod and approves of the conclusions reached, such a congress will be ecumenical. Finally, however, the Pope may preside through the medium of his delegates, who in his name and by his authority are qualified to direct the convocation and to approve the acts according to the tenor of the mandate by which they have been commissioned.[18]

The last mentioned manner of presiding over a general synod has been most common throughout the course of history. It affords clearly an illustration of delegation. Such legates are commissioned to bear the person and the authority of the Pope, and indeed for a particular and transitory negotiation, so that in no way can their office be regarded as a permanent institution, or their power as ordinary. For this reason it will be profitable to present a few of the more important historical instances of this method.

The First Ecumenical Council, held at Nicaea in 325, was presided over by Hosius, Bishop of Cordova, and by Vitus and Vincentius, priests of Rome, as delegates of the Holy See. This is testified to by Gelasius, a historian of the fifth century,[19] and by the writer Socrates;[20] while Theodoret [21] at least notes that the Bishop of Rome sent to the Synod two priests. The position of the signatures of the three representatives of Rome indicates

---

[15] Hefele-Clarke, *A History of the Christian Councils*, I, 27.

[16] Tanquerey, *Brevior Synopsis Theologiae Dogmaticae*, p. 143.

[17] Hardouin, III, 218-44; 213-18; cf. Hefele-Clarke, *op. cit.*, I, 14.

[18] Tanquerey, *op. cit.*, p. 143; Hefele-Clarke, *op. cit.*, I, 27.

[19] Gelasii Cyziceni Commentarius, II, 5—Mansi, II, 806.

[20] *Historia Ecclesiastica*, I, 13—*MPG* LXVII, 110.

[21] *Historia Ecclesiastica*, I, cap. 6.

the function they performed; their names are found before those of the patriarchs of the East, although one was the bishop of an insignificant Spanish See, and the others only priests. In the list prepared by Mansi [22] the name of Hosius appears without further annotation. The very uniqueness of this is significant, since all other bishops are signed according to their respective provincial groups. The names, however, of the two Roman priests are qualified explicitly by what is already implicit in the name of Hosius, for with their names is read, "We, Victor and Vincentius, priests of Rome, have affixed our names for the venerable S. Silvester, our Pope and Bishop, so believing, as it has been written." [23]

The Council of Nicaea, therefore, affords an early example of the institution with which this paper is concerned. The office of the legates expired when they had returned to Rome; while it endured, they wielded an authority over the prelates of highest rank who were in attendance at the Synod. This authority could have been nothing less than pontifical. It is evident that no one who is not a pope, can exercise such authority, unless he is conceived as a delegate of one who enjoys such jurisdiction in his own right.

The presidency of Nicaea was no exception. Many subsequent councils were directed in a like manner. The Third General Council was convoked to combat the growing disease of Nestorianism, and Cyril was chosen as the champion of Rome in this time of strife.[24] Cyril was obviously the president of the first session, held at Ephesus in 431; his name is placed before all others with the annotation that he "took the place of Celestine, the most holy Archbishop of Rome." [25] At the second session Cyril was joined by Arcadius and Projectus, bishops, and the priest Philippus, who had been instructed to act in unison with Cyril.[26] All these signed the acts as delegates of the Holy See.[27]

The Fourth General Council was held at Chalcedon in 451

---

[22] II, 692; 697; 882; 927.

[23] Hardouin, I, 311.

[24] Hardouin, I, 1323.

[25] Hardouin, I, 1353; cf. 1486; 1510.

[26] Hardouin, I, 1347; 1473.

[27] Hardouin, I, 402; 451; II, 671; 742; III, 10; 1052.

to refute the heresy of Eutyches.[28] In June of that year Leo announced to Anatolius his intention of sending representatives to the Synod, and later in a letter to the Synod he expressed regret that he could not attend personally. He wrote, however, "In these my brothers Paschasinus and Lucentius, Bishops, and in Boniface and Basil, priests, who have been dispatched from the Apostolic See, you, my brethren, will regard me to preside, for I shall be there in my vicars."[29] At the same time Leo ordered Julian of Cos to be present, "making use of the weight of our authority."[30] And later, writing to the bishops of Gaul, Leo referred to these legates as "my brothers, who presided in my place over the Oriental Synod."[31] Finally in the third session Paschasinus announced that he and his colleagues had been ordered to preside in behalf of the Roman Pontiff.[32]

At the Sixth General Council, held at Constantinople (680-681), the first to subscribe were Theodore, George and John, legates of the Holy See.[33] At the Seventh Council (787) the Archpresbyter Peter and the Abbot Peter represented the Pope;[34] while Donatus, Bishop of Ostia, Stephen, Bishop of Nepesina, and Marinus represented Hadrian II at the Eighth Council, held at Constantinople 869-870.[35] These legates evidently directed the entire movement of the Synod, despite the fact that the Emperor Basil was present, as is revealed in a later epistle of Hadrian to the Emperor in which the Pope commends the latter for being present, not as a judge of the proceedings, but as a spectator and protector.[36]

The facts mentioned are sufficient to illustrate one manner of delegation that has figured prominent in church history. In every case the legates of the Pope have enjoyed in a transitory manner an authority that cannot properly be conceived

---

[28] Funk, *A Manual of Church History*, I, 158.

[29] Ep. ad Synodum quae . . . Chalcedone congregata est—Mansi, VI, 134.

[30] Ep. ad Julianum Coensem—Mansi, VI, 131.

[31] Ep. ad Episcopos Galliarum—*MPL* LIV, 988.

[32] Hardouin, II, 310.

[33] Hardouin, III, 1055. Cf. 1061; 1065; 1624.

[34] Hardouin, IV, 28 ss.

[35] Hardouin, V, 764.

[36] Hardouin, V, 939; Hefele-Clarke, *A History of the Christian Councils*, I, 29.

as their own, since they exercised a preeminence over prelates of the highest rank. These are clear instances of delegated power.

§4. *Delegated Judicial Power*

An additional evidence of apostolic delegation, essentially different from that related above, is found in the Council of Sardica, convened in 343. Specifically, the Council was interested in judicial controversies that might arise between two bishops. The third canon of the Council directs that such a matter should be seen by a provincial synod, without any intervention on the part of foreign bishops. It prescribes that, if a bishop, unsuccessful in the first judicial instance, sees fit to appeal, he may do so to the Pope, who will constitute a tribunal composed of neighboring bishops, or, as the merits of the case demand, ratify the first sentence.[37]

The fifth canon, however, proceeds further. It treats of a bishop who has been condemned to the specific penalty of deposition; and it establishes a specific remedy. It states:

> If he who asks that his case be heard, induces the Bishop of Rome to send from his court a presbyter, the Pope will be free to do what he wishes and what he deems best; and if he decides to send some endowed with the authority of him by whom they are sent, who together with the bishops may pass judgment, in this too will he be free.[38]

This canon asserted the right of the Holy See to nominate judges who together with the usual tribunal of bishops would pass sentence in the second instance. It further made clear the nature of the jurisdiction which such judges would enjoy, for they will be "endowed with the authority of him by whom they are sent." They would be, therefore, truly delegates of the Holy See, not exercising their own proper jurisdiction, but that of the Bishop of Rome.

This particular disposition so effectively refutes the contentions of the adversaries, that they have devoted special efforts to frustrate the validity of the argument. Febronius [39] has

---

[37] Hefele-Clarke, *A History of the Christian Councils*, II, 112 ss.

[38] Hefele-Clarke, *op. cit.*, II, 120.

[39] *De Statu Ecclesiae et Legitima Potestate Romani Pontificis*, cap. V, V, p. 259 ss.

contended that here there was no question of a true appeal in the juridical sense of the term, but that the canon signified a mere revision. To substantiate this claim he has argued that after a true judicial appeal the judges of the second instance may never be the same as those of the first instance; the canons in question, however, do not exclude the judges of the first hearing from the second session.

This deduction is not correct. The fifth canon must be taken in conjunction with the third, by virtue of which the second tribunal will be composed of bishops of a *neighboring province*, and it is to these that the delegated judges of the Pope will be associated. In the first instance the case would have been seen by the bishops of the defendant's own province. Thus the judges of the second process necessarily would be different from those of the first.

Moreover, a mere revision is out of the question. The Council dealt with a most consequential matter, the deposition of a bishop. Such a matter demanded a most effective and decisive remedy. A mere revision would be an inane procedure in such a crisis. Furthermore, the entire tenor of the canon is judicial; and the word employed is technical for appeal.[40] Finally, it may be noted that during this appeal, no other bishop may be elevated to the place vacated by the defendant, as the fourth canon prescribes.[41] Such a suspension of execution always indicates an appeal in the strictest juridical sense.[42]

Subsequent events justify this interpretation of the canons examined. During the reign of Zosimus (417-418), the priest Apiarius of proconsular Africa, deposed and excommunicated by his bishop, appealed to the Holy See. The Pope adjudged the case contrary to the first sentence rendered, and ordered the reinstatement of the priest. The bishops of Africa, displeased with this result, decreed in a general synod:

> If priests, deacons and inferior clerics complain of a sentence imposed by their bishop, they shall have recourse, with the consent of their bishop, to the neighboring bishops, who will settle the dispute. If they desire to make higher

---

40 ἐκκαλεσάμενος ; cf. Hefele-Clarke, *op. cit.*, II, 124; Stephanus, *Thesaurus Graecae Linguae*, IV, v. καλέω

41 Hefele-Clarke, *op. cit.*, II, 116.

42 Hefele-Clarke, *op. cit.*, II, 128.

> appeal, it must be only to their primates or to African councils. But whosoever appeals to a court on the other side of the sea (Rome), may not be received again into communion by anyone in Africa.[43]

Thereupon, the Pope sent to Carthage Faustinus, Philip and Asellus.[44] Faustinus, on behalf of the Pope, quoted the canons on appeal from the Council of Sardica, but he erroneously claimed them to be Nicene canons.[45] This error was owing to the fact that the canons of subsequent synods were usually adjoined to those of Nicaea, and were not always distinguishable from them.[46] Because of this error the African bishops were unable to trace the canons quoted. So great indeed was their respect for the Holy See, represented by Faustinus, that they agreed to observe the canons until such a time as they might be demonstrated to be spurious.[47]

Appreciable space has been devoted to the proof that the question was one of true appeal, and not any purely administrative process. If indeed there was question of judicial appeal, the delegates sent by the Pope to review the case were clearly endowed with judicial jurisdiction. This is an important fact in the history of delegation.

Another example of delegation in judicial matters is evidenced during the reign of Sixtus III (432-440), at which time Athanasius was the incumbent of the permanent legation established at Thessalonica. The Pope informed the bishops of this region that any dispute arising among them should be submitted to Athanasius, "who is known to fill the office of the Holy See according to our will"; that if a settlement could not thus be reached, the matter could be sent to Rome, in which case the Vicar of Thessalonica would be obliged to transmit in writing his own opinion.[48] At the same time the Pope made clear that the legate had full authority to delegate others who might assist in such affairs, when he wrote, "Let him choose

---

[43] Hefele-Clarke, *op. cit.*, II, 461.
[44] Mansi, IV, 403; 405.
[45] Mansi, III, 831.
[46] Hefele-Clarke, *op. cit.*, I, 356 ss.
[47] Hefele-Clarke, *op. cit.*, II, 464; 457.
[48] Ep. ad Episcopos per Illyricum consistentes—Mansi, VIII, 762.

excellent and skilful men from your number, whom he may join with himself as arbiters for the matters at hand."[49]

A final specimen of this type of delegation may be proposed from a case occurring under Gelasius (492-96). Sabinus had ordained Antiochus to the priesthood and Leonicus to the clericate, both of whom were slaves, during the absence of their mistress and without her consent. Now, such an ordination was gravely illicit, as may be seen in the *Canones Apostolorum*, since a serious injustice was thus inflicted on the owner of the slaves, who could no longer retain them in their low state of life.[50] Gelasius designated for this unique case Herculentius, Stephen and Justus as his delegated judges, and his letters make clear that he conceded to them ample power to punish the delinquent bishop, should justice so demand.[51]

§5. *The Vicariate of Thessalonica*

It is well known that the Popes have been wont to attach permanently to some sees the office of Papal Legate.[52] It is not an easy matter to determine the nature of the power exercised by the incumbents of these offices. It is certain that they labored in the name of the Roman Pontiff; and in this respect their power would be regarded as vicarious. Under the legislation of the Code such power must be accepted as ordinary.[53] Canonists, however, for many centuries have been at a loss as to the true nature of vicarious power. Before the Code it was more commonly regarded as a form of delegated power, rather than ordinary.[54] There was much to sustain this opinion, since he who was endowed with such power, functioned in the name of another who enjoyed it by native right, and the vicar was conceived as entirely dependent on him in whose name he operated. This intimate connection between the vicar and the ordinary officer might easily be confused with a simple notion

[49] Ep. ad Episcopos Synodo apud Thessalonicam congregandos—Mansi, VIII, 761.

[50] Can. 81—Hardouin, I, 19.

[51] C. 10, D. 54.

[52] V.g., Thessalonica, Arles, Sicily, Seville, Tarraco; cf. Pius VI, *Responsio ad Metropolitanos*, p. 227.

[53] Can. 197, §2.

[54] Wernz, II, n. 686.

of delegation, or commission, deriving from one to the other. When the Code finally put an end to this controversy, the theoretical question was not decided in one way or the other, but a mere practical norm was established for the legislation contained in the Code, which at the same time made useless any prolongation of the old discussion. In the light, therefore, of the old legislation the power enjoyed by the permanent vicars attached to the privileged sees may be regarded as delegated, if it is permissible to adjudge historical facts in the light of the jurisprudence that was contemporary to them.

The value of the permanent legates in the present study is apparent likewise from other considerations. In the first place, many ecclesiastical offices became such by virtue of a gradual transition from an initial delegation.[55] This fact is well exemplified in the case of the archdeacons and archpresbyters.[56] It is quite likely that the same is true of the permanent legates; only in the course of time could they naturally acquire a certain degree of independence and individual stability. In the meantime, they were but delegates of the Supreme Pontiff. Furthermore, such legates were very probably delegates, since the concept of delegate is more basic and more natural than that of vicar. In the early periods of church history, with which this paper is here concerned, ecclesiastics were not interested in theoretical niceties, but rather in attaining practical results. There was no question raised with regard to the intricacies that would be involved in a discussion as to the nature of the power committed, and the more natural concept may be presumed to have prevailed. It is not, therefore, unreasonable to urge as specimens of apostolic delegation, at least in the first centuries, the permanent vicariates established in distant regions in order that these might more effectively be in communion with the primatial See.

Of all the permanent vicariates, that of Thessalonica was by far the most ancient. Innocent I (401-417) in appointing Rufus to this dignity declared that he was "imitating his apostolic successors."[57] Again he spoke in almost the same

---

[55] Maroto, *Institutiones,* I, n. 700.

[56] Wernz, II, n. 545; 686.

[57] Ep. ad Rufum—Mansi, VIII, 751.

terms when he committed to Anysius most ample powers.[58] Pope Boniface likewise testifies to the antiquity of this legation, for in naming a new vicar he states that he follows the example of Christ Himself and the custom of those whom already in the fifth century he calls *fathers*.[59] Sixtus III likewise testifies to the antiquity of this institution when he says, "We concede to our brother and cobishop Anastasius as much as was attributed to his predecessors by those who preceded us. We follow the prudence of the *ancients* in maintaining what we know were established by them."[60] Thomassinus states of this vicariate, "Damasus and Sirycius laid the first foundations of the apostolic vicariate of Thessalonica; but Innocent I imposed the crown."[61]. The standing of this legation is further evidenced in a dispute that occurred during the reign of Pope Boniface. The bishops of Illyria complained to the Emperor, stating that they preferred to be subject to the Patriarch of Constantinople rather than to the Bishop of Thessalonica. The Emperor then enacted a law which favored the complaint of the bishops. When, however, the Pope protested, the Emperor receded from his position and wrote to Honorius, "We have decided that what the ancient apostolic discipline and canons prescribe, is to be observed. . . . Therefore have we written, that the bishops, desisting from their deceit, in a special manner see that the old order is preserved."[62]

The contention that the faculties of this most ancient legation were delegated is confirmed by the writings of Pius VI.[63] The Pontiff first tells of the ample powers enjoyed by the Vicar, and then he adds, "That the theme may be more orderly, we shall distinguish faculties which are of ordinary jurisdiction from those which are called of contentious jurisdiction, lest we wander even by a trifle from the Pontifical letters, which are *certain and indubious monuments of delegated*

[58] Ep. ad Anysium—Mansi, VIII, 750.

[59] "Audio enim episcoporum quosdam apostolico jure contempto novum quidquam contra Christi praecepta tentare. . . . Nullus ea, quae sunt a *Patribus* gesta et per tantum temporis custodita, temerare contendat." Ep. ad Episcopos per Thessaliam constitutos—Mansi, VIII, 755.

[60] Ep. ad Episcopos Synodo apud Thessalonicam congregandos—Mansi, VIII, 761.

[61] *Vetus et Nova Ecclesiae Disciplina*, lib. I, cap. 18, n. 7.

[62] Rescriptum Theodosii ad Honorium—*MPL* XX, 770; 778.

[63] *Responsio ad Metropolitanos*, cap. VIII, sec. III, p. 210.

power." The Pope here places in contraposition ordinary and contentious power; hence, in his mind, ordinary power must correspond to the administrative power of modern law, since this alone is opposed to the contentious. At the same time he classifies them all as *monuments of delegated power.*

These few observations made with regard to the nature of the power of the Vicar of Thessalonica may be extended to the permanent vicars set up in the other legations. All of these were modelled after the most ancient of all vicariates and were endowed in a similar manner with prerogatives that were Papal in character.

§6. *Types of Legates*

The vicars of the permanent vicariates have been called *legati nati*; those who were sent for a particular mission or occasion have been termed *legati a latere* and *legati missi.*[64] The name *legatus a latere,* however, has usually been reserved to those who have proceeded from the Pope on a mission of a very important character and only for a brief period. The term *legatus missus* has more regularly denoted those who, although not permanently constituted in an official capacity, have represented the person of the Pope for a longer period or for a greater number of matters. Such were the Responsales and Apocrisaries who dwelled at the courts of the Emperors in the interests of the Holy See. A few instances of legates of either type may be presented here to advance the study with which the present chapter is concerned.

The Arians had done much to discredit Athanasius at Constantinople and wished to effect the same at Rome. Pope Liberius deemed it necessary to examine thoroughly the charges and consequently he sent legates to Constantius who was wintering at Arles (353-4). He sent, therefore, Vincent, Bishop of Capua, and Marcellus, Bishop of Campania.[65] These legates assisted at a synod at Arles, and much to the grief of the Pope they subscribed to a condemnation of Athanasius. A second synod was called at Milan (355) through the instrumentality of Lucifer, Bishop of Cagliari, and his colleagues, Pancratius

---

[64] Devoti, *Jus Universum,* lib. I, tit. XXX, p. 270.

[65] Ep. ad Osium Cordubensem—Mansi, III, 200.

and Hilary.[66] Later these were joined by Eusebius of Vercelli.[67] This entire group of legates was finally exiled because of its fidelity to the Holy See. At another date this same Eusebius was a supporter of Athanasius at the Council of Alexandria. It was of him in part that Thomassinus wrote, "Neither of these leaders could have exercised in the Orient so great a jurisdiction without delegation from the primatial See." [68]

During the reign of Leo (440-461) innumerable delegations were conceded. In committing a group of churches to Anastasius the Pontiff wrote, that he did so in imitation of Siricius who had entrusted them to Anysius.[69] At the same time in his letter to the bishops he showed the dignity which characterized the representatives of the Holy See, saying, "In those matters which pertain to ecclesiastical discipline we exhort you to obey him; for thus, not he, but we, shall be obeyed, who are known in our solicitude to have entrusted to him our care over those provinces." [70] Indeed, so conscious was Anastasius of the tremendous authority he bore, that it became needful later to call him to task for exceeding prudence in exercising it.[71]

The authority of the legates is made manifest likewise in the letter of Leo to the Emperor Marcian, delegating Julian, Bishop of Cos, to safeguard the faith against the Christological errors, when he says, "I have delegated to him my office against the heretics of our time; and for the custody of the churches and of peace I have urged that he be not distant from thee. Do thou deign to hear his suggestions as though they were mine." [72]

§7. *Subdelegation*

By the term subdelegation is understood nothing more than mediate delegation. It is essentially the same as delegation, or the commitment of one's own power to another. It is distinguished from simple delegation as the mediate is distinguished

[66] Mansi, III, 202.
[67] Ep. ad Eusebium Vercel.—Mansi, III, 204.
[68] *Vetus et Nova Ecclesiae Disciplina,* lib. II, cap. 117, p. 824.
[69] Ep. ad Anastasium—Mansi, V, 1133.
[70] Ep. ad Metropolitanos per Illyricum constitutos—Mansi, V, 1130.
[71] Ep. ad Anastasium—Mansi, V, 1178.
[72] Ep. ad Marcianum Augustum—Mansi, VI, 217.

from the immediate. In subdelegation the commitment of power is effected by one who does not enjoy the power in his own name or by his own right, but by one who in his turn has received it from another who does enjoy it by native right. In the early periods of church history examples of such mediate delegation are not entirely lacking.

The letters of commission given to Rufus by Innocent I in appointing him to the Vicariate of Thessalonica afford a very probable instance of such. In preceding pages the contention has been that the Vicar was truly a delegate. To this Vicar Innocent gave the faculty of choosing bishops from the various churches, who together with himself might constitute a tribunal and pass sentence, whenever need might arise.[73] Since the arbiters thus chosen would not have of themselves the jurisdiction necessary, and since no further recourse to Rome is even insinuated as necessary for the acquisition of authority, it is to be concluded that the Papal Legate had it in his power to communicate to those of his choosing the same jurisdiction which he himself possessed—that of the Supreme Pontiff.

Pope Sixtus III (432-440) confirms this observation, for in mentioning the judicial character of the Vicar of Thessalonica, he too speaks of the faculty of the Vicar to join to himself experienced men, as judges, when occasion demands.[74]

Article II—Delegation Among Inferior Prelates

The historical facts presented in the preceding pages have been centered exclusively about the Supreme Pontiff. Naturally, literary monuments of the first centuries are concerned primarily with the Head of all Christianity, and they relate little that deals with the more minute details of church government. From this, however, it must not be deduced that delegation was limited only to the sphere of pontifical affairs. Delegation was an instrument of good government and was undoubtedly used by inferiors as well as by the Apostolic See. The beginnings of any great organization postulate the use of

---

[73] Ep. ad Rufum—Mansi, VIII, 751.

[74] Ep. ad Episcopos Synodo apud Thessalonicam congregandos—Mansi, VIII, 761.

such a method. The pioneers of Christianity retained under their own control and vigilance those who blazed the way for the faith in missionary places. Only when these subordinates had attained a certain degree of stability in respective territories, may they be conceived as laboring in their own name, by their own right, and with only a remote dependence on their superiors.

It is reasonable to conclude that the inferior clergy, who in the course of time became the regular incumbents of ecclesiastical offices, were in the beginning mere agents of the bishops and presbyters. Wernz states substantially the same, when he says, "Bishops too were not without their vicars, among whom are worthy of particular mention the Archdeacons and Archpresbyters and those rural priests (later pastors), who from the first centuries exercised the care of souls outside the city. All these became *ordinary* magistrates gradually."[75] The present parochial system, as Wernz has suggested, had its origin in these rural priests, so that already in the sixth century it had found its way into many regions and nations.[76]

Besides the clerics already mentioned, the chorbishops of the East represent a similar evolution. These prelates were rural bishops, as the name implies.[77] So numerous were bishops in the early part of the fourth century, that the Council of Sardica saw fit to prohibit the consecration of them in the future in small towns and villages.[78] The office of chorbishop, like the others, began, no doubt, by individual commissions and evolved gradually into stable ecclesiastical magistracies.[79]

Article III—Conclusion

The preceding chapter has brought into evidence many historical instances of delegation, none of which have been taken from a period later than the fifth century. This very fact is sufficient to refute effectively the contentions of the adversaries who held that Papal jurisdiction had never been exercised out-

75 II, n. 545.

76 Chelodi, *Jus de Personis*, p. 338; Zaplotnik, *De Vicariis Foraneis*, p. 14.

77 Χώρας ἐπίσκοποι; cf. Hefele-Clarke, *A History of the Christian Councils*, I, 17; *Devoti, Institutionum Canonicarum Libri IV*, I, 167.

78 Can. VII—Hefele-Clarke, *op. cit.*, I, 129.

79 Thomassinus, *Vetus et Nova Ecclesiae Disciplina*, Lib. II, cap. I, n. 15.

side the See of Rome until after the pseudo-Isidoran decretals had produced their full effect.

It must be noted that the canonical institution of delegation during the period just reviewed has not been developed scientifically. The fact of delegation has been established and the dignity and authority of the delegate has been evidenced. It is clear that the delegate is the *Alter Ego* of the person whom he represents; the delegate bears the person of his commissioner and as such, regardless of his native rights, takes precedence over all who are not as high in rank as he whom the delegate impersonates. So much of the nature of delegation is inescapable in this early period.

Evidences of subdelegation have also been revealed. Further principles are not manifested by the limited data at hand concerning the first centuries of the church. This does not imply that restrictions and limitations were not affixed to the communication of power, since even in Roman law such were recognized. It remained for the history of subsequent centuries to tell what the history of primitive Christianity suppressed in silence.

CHAPTER III

History of Delegation to the Council of Trent

Article I—Period Before Trent

It would be at best an unprofitable labor to bring into evidence the innumerable instances of delegation that mark the path of ecclesiastical history after the fifth century. The Church continued to grow extensively and ecclesiastical negotiations kept apace. The Popes continued to make use of the services of trusted men for important affairs, just as in the preceding periods. The evolution of delegation as a canonical instrument is not marked for some centuries; not until the period of the decretals is any light cast upon the principles that governed the communication of jurisdiction. It may be permissible to offer a very few examples of delegation that will serve to establish a period of transition to a time when the full force of delegation becomes apparent.

§1. *Apostolic Legates*

Pope Hormisdas (514-523) thus commissioned John, a Bishop, "With due observance of the privileges of the Metropolitans, we delegate to you the faculties of the Apostolic See, so that what has recently been decreed by us, may be carried out; and whatever may come to your knowledge concerning ecclesiastical affairs, you may make known to us."[1] Pope Gregory (590-604) is known to have committed to Antoninus, a subdeacon, extensive power over certain cases, reserving to himself only the most arduous matters.[2] And again the same Pontiff wrote to the subdeacon Peter, "We have deemed it quite necessary that we commit to one and the same person all power, so that where we cannot be present, our authority may be repre-

[1] C. 6, C. XXV, q. 2.

[2] Jaffée, n. 1205.

sented by one whom we have designated. Wherefore, to Peter, a subdeacon of our see, we have, by the grace of God, committed our care over the province of Sicily. . . . We cannot be hesitant concerning the acts of one to whom we are known to have entrusted the entire heritage of the church." [3]

Boniface, the Apostle of Germany, labored as representative of the Holy See during the pontificates of four Popes. On one occasion Gregory III ordered Boniface to hold a synod in the region of the Danube, and the Pope proclaimed him as his delegate.[4] At a later date Boniface asked Pope Zachary (741-752) to send an extraordinary legate who would convoke a synod in Gaul; to which the Pope responded, "While your holiness yet survives and represents the office of the Holy See and our office, it is unnecessary to send another." [5]

Peter Damian was often employed as the instrument of the Holy See. Nicholas II (1058-1061) sent him to Milan to act against a corrupt clergy. Damian, sitting as delegate of the Pope, punished even the Archbishop, a fact that makes clear the nature of the power he wielded.[6] Later Alexander II (1061-1073) sent him to France, writing at the same time to the bishops of that nation that Damian was to be considered as bearing the person and authority of the Supreme Pontiff.[7]

These facts are sufficient to establish an uninterrupted link in the history of delegation. Development of principles is not yet possible historically. What follows can elucidate the norms of the past and establish a system for the future legislation of the church.

§2. *The Period of Decretal Law*

During the period of the Decretals delegation as a canonical institute attained its pre-Code perfection. Principles had been formulated in the course of time as occasion demanded, and all were gathered together by the efforts of Gregory IX. It is to be noted, however, that the principles of delegation as embodied in the *Decretals* refer exclusively to delegated judges. In this

[3] C. 1, D. 84; Jaffée, n. 1067.
[4] Ep. ad Bonifacium—Mansi, XII, 285.
[5] Ep. ad Bonifacium—Mansi, XII, 342.
[6] *MPL* CXLV, 90.
[7] Ep. ad archiepiscopos Galliae—*MPL* CXLVI, 1295.

period ecclesiastical courts functioned frequently and enjoyed extensive competence. It is in consequence to this fact that Pontiffs often were compelled to declare authentically a principle with regard to the acquisition, extent or cessation of delegation in judicial matters. Alexander III, Lucius III, Coelestine III, Innocent III, and Gregory IX have by their legislations inscribed their names deeply into the development of this institution. Their ordinances regarding the delegated judge have constituted a distinct title in the Decretals of Gregory IX.[8]

A half-century after the death of Gregory, Boniface VIII (1294-1303) assumed the Papal throne. This Pontiff contributed largely to the science of canon law in general by the composition of his *Liber Sextus,* in which a distinct title is likewise devoted to the delegated judge.[9] But again, the principles of delegation are restricted to one sphere, and general principles are not advanced.

It would be superfluous to reproduce in these pages even the more important steps of progress, indicated in Decretal Law. They are all, with few exceptions, embodied in the Code of 1918, which has deduced from them a group of general principles, applicable to every species of power that admits of commission to others. In treating of the canons of the Code, the writer will attempt more opportunely to indicate whatever changes have been brought about in the law of the Decretals by the most recent ecclesiastical legislation.

Article II—The Council of Trent

The Council of Trent has bequeathed two important monuments to the history of delegation. The first regards synodal judges; the second pertains to a frequent delegation *a iure* by which bishops acquired the faculty of acting in certain affairs as delegates of the Holy See. A brief word about each of these will be of advantage.

§1. *Synodal Judges*

For some centuries judicial cases referred to Rome were entrusted to ecclesiastics who habitually dwelled in the Roman

[8] *De officio et potestate iudicis delegati,* I, 29.

[9] *De officio et potestate iudicis delegati,* I, 14 in Sext.

Curia with the title of Papal Chaplains (Cappellani Papales). More frequently, however, such cases were submitted to judges distributed throughout the various sees, who discerned the affairs by virtue of delegated jurisdiction of the Holy See. One species of such delegates was the *Judex Conservator*. It was his duty to defend especially the unfortunate against manifest injuries and violences.[10] Forti [11] has indicated eight differences, however, between the usual delegated judge and the *Conservator*, among which is worthy of particular mention the exclusion of a faculty to subdelegate.

This system was not without its difficulties. Because of the great distances between sees and the difficulty attendant upon communication in that period, it happened not infrequently that the Pope knew little or nothing concerning the persons who were enjoying Papal jurisdiction; as a result incapable and unqualified persons sometimes were in possession of high authority.

In order that the Holy See might be represented by persons worthy of such an honorable office, Boniface VIII decreed that in the future no person might fulfill this function unless he was a canon of a cathedral church or was endowed with an ecclesiastical dignity or possessed of a personate. He further prohibited the hearing of such cases by virtue of Papal delegation except in great cities or celebrated places, where the services of skilled jurists and the testimony of experts, if required, might be procured.[12] This restriction further tended to the avoidance of simony, since the judges thus qualified were already in possession of a lucrative benefice, and judicial processes could more safely be rendered gratuitously.[13]

Such legislation gained perfection and stability in the Council of Trent. The Fathers prescribed that in every provincial council or diocesan synod there should be chosen at least four judges for each diocese; that the judges so selected should be endowed with the qualifications set forth by Boniface VIII, and

---

[10] Ferraris, *Bibliotheca*, v. Conservatores; Forti, *De Judice Conservatore Regularium*, art. I.

[11] *Op. cit.*, art. I, n. 29-38.

[12] C. 11, *de rescriptis*, I, 3, in Sext.; c. 15, *de officio et potestate iudicis delegati*, I, 14, in Sext.; Noval, *De Judiciis*, p. 62; Roberti, *De Processibus*, I, n. 101; Lega, *De Judiciis Ecclesiasticis*, n. 68.

[13] Lega, *op. cit.*, n. 68.

also with those natural and acquired faculties that would make one fit for such an office; and that those elected should be called *Judices Synodales.* They further ordained that in the case of the death of any of these officers before the convocation of another synod, the Ordinary with the consent of his Chapter should appoint substitutes who would be called *Judices Pro-Synodales.*[14]

On August 26, 1741, Benedict XIV in his constitution *Quamvis Paternae* reiterated the provisions of the Council and made further opportune arrangements. Realizing that in some regions synods rarely were convened, he decreed that in such places the bishops or archbishops would select the judges, and he imposed on these prelates the obligation of registering the names of the appointed in the Roman Curia.[15]

The synodal judge did not possess a permanent and constant ecclesiastical function. He was merely a qualified and approved officer to whom the Holy See might with confidence commit judicial matters that had been brought to her forum for decision. With the development of the Roman Curia the need of such officers was diminished considerably, so that such affáirs became matter for the Roman congregations, tribunals and offices, or were transmitted to the ordinaries as delegates of the Holy See.[16] The synodal judge, however, has found a new title to existence in the recent codification. He is no longer an officer of the Holy See; but he is a diocesan judge who by virtue of episcopal delegation constitutes with the Official the ordinary diocesan tribunal.[17]

§2. *Bishops as Apostolic Delegates*

Lucius III (1181-1185) had set a precedent by which bishops were empowered to act as delegates of the Holy See.[18] Other Pontiffs subsequently adapted the same method of procedure to meet growing difficulties.[19] Such provisions enabled the

---

[14] Conc. Trent, Sess. XXV, de ref., c. 10.

[15] *Fontes,* n. 315.

[16] Roberti, *op. cit.,* n. 101; Lega, *op. cit.,* n. 68.

[17] Can. 1574; Roberti, *op. cit.,* n. 101.

[18] C. 9, X, *de haereticis,* V, 7.

[19] C. 13, X, *de officio iudicis ordinarii,* I, 31; c. un., *de supplenda neglegentia praelatorum,* I, 5 in Clem.; c. 2, *de statu monach.,* III, 10 in Clem.

bishops to proceed against the exempt in matters that ordinarily were reserved to the Holy See. Thus prompt action, which frequently is of prime importance in the infliction of penalties, was made possible, without the necessity of recourse to the distant See of Rome, at least in the first instance. The Council of Trent approved of this method of procedure and increased to a much greater number the applications of the same.

Two formulas are found in the decrees of the Council, the first of which empowered the bishops to act *as Delegates of the Apostolic See.*[20] By this clause a power was conceded to the bishops which they did not enjoy before. A notable effect of such procedure was the necessity of making appeal directly to the Roman Pontiff, and not to the Metropolitan, as from delegate to delegator.[21] Furthermore, such delegated power did not pass over to the *Capitulum* of the cathedral church on the occasion of the vacancy of the see, as did the episcopal ordinary power.[22]

The second formula used frequently in the Council of Trent enabled the bishops to act *also as Delegates of the Apostolic See.*[23] The force of this clause is not so easily explained, and has been the cause of keen dispute between the older canonists. The word *etiam* insinuates that the bishops already enjoyed some ordinary competence in such matters over their own subjects, not withdrawn from their jurisdiction by the privilege of exemption.[24] The majority of canonists have, therefore, regarded the effect of the clause in question as the cumulation of Papally delegated jurisdiction and the ordinary jurisdiction of a bishop.[25] By force, then, of this clause the bishops could act by virtue of either ordinary or delegated power, as they preferred. In doubt they were presumed to have acted by Papal authority, since this was more honorable and appeal was made

---

20 *Tamquam Apostolicae Sedis Delegati.* Cf. sess. VI, de ref., cap. 3; sess. V, de ref., cap. 1, 2; sess. XXIV, de ref., cap. 9, 11, 14; sess. XXV, de reg., cap. 8, 9; et passim.

21 Reiffenstuel, lib. I, tit. XXIX, n. 36; DeAngelis, *Praelectiones,* I, 116.

22 Wernz, II, 695.

23 *Etiam tamquam Apostolicae Sedis Delegati.* Cf. sess. V, de ref., cap. 2; sess. XXI, de ref., cap 3-8; sess. XXV, de reg., cap. 5.

24 Wernz, II, 696.

25 Maroto, *Institutiones,* I, p. 842, not. 1; Reiffenstuel, lib. I, tit. XXIX, n. 37; Wernz, II, 696; Santi, *Praelectiones,* lib. I, tit. XXIX, n. 3.

less frequent.[26] In addition to this faculty of acting against their own proper subjects by either of a twofold power, they could also act against the exempt in the cases contemplated by the law.[27]

Hinschius[28] and many of the German canonists[29] have not agreed with this traditional interpretation. They have regarded the power thus conferred by the Council of Trent as merely the faculty to act against the exempt, and not at all a cumulation of power that could be exercised at will against the proper non-exempt subjects of the bishops.

This dispute is now a matter of history. The Code, if it has not excluded all delegations *a iure* from the present legislation, as some contend, has at least reduced the number of the same to a minimum; but, more definitely, the Code has discontinued the use of the distinction between bishops as delegates, and bishops *also* as delegates of the Holy See. Because of abuses many bishops desired a total abolition of exemption. The Fathers of the Council steered a middle course; they empowered the bishops to act as Papal delegates over the exempt in certain matters, and at the same time the privilege of exemption was sustained.[30]

Article III—Post-Tridentine Legislation

After the Council of Trent, and until 1918, decretal law remained in force. The principles regarding delegation as set forth in the Decretals were the practical norms of canonical usage, although they were entirely too specific to be adapted to the generality of law.

There can be no doubt as to the frequency of the use of delegation during this period. The tremendous missionary activity of the church in recent centuries was the occasion of the concession of very extensive faculties to the Vicars and Prefects Apostolic, as well as to those inferior clerics who carried

---

[26] Ojetti, *Synopsis*, v. *Delegatio*, n. 1732-4; Reiffenstuel, lib. I, tit. XXIX, n. 38.

[27] Wernz, II, n. 696; Badii, *Institutiones*, p. 131, not. 2.

[28] *System des Katholischen Kirchenrechts*, I, 177.

[29] Cf. Stutz, *Der Geist des Codex Iuris Canonici*, p. 270.

[30] Wernz, II, n. 695.

the cross of Christianity into unexplored fields.[31] A glance at the faculties which are even now granted by the Holy See to Nuntios, Internuntios, Delegates, Ordinaries and missionaries, will reveal how frequent an application the principles regarding delegation must find in the normal and constant life of the church.[32]

The legislation of the past in regard to the principles of which this paper treats, was far from perfect. The efficient administration of Christ's church demanded a new and scientific codification of law. This was realized little more than a decade ago. The *Codex Iuris Canonici* was the answer to the difficulty. In the Code the principles of delegation are presented in a brief, concise, scientific treatise, that is applicable to the entire material capable of commission to others. The chapters that follow will attempt to cast some light on these principles as embodied in the Code.

---

31 Wernz-Vidal, *Jus Canonicum,* II, 363.

32 Vermeersch-Creusen, *Epitome,* I, p. 523, append. I-III.

PART II—COMMENTARY

CHAPTER IV

The Concept of Delegation

The historical study that has preceded, affords a notion of the various elements that enter into the concept of delegation. It would be futile to proffer as a definition of delegation the descriptions that are found among even the classical writers on Canon Law. The promulgation of the Code is the high-water mark in the history of ecclesiastical law. That event, in very many instances, is the dividing line between the authentic and the obsolete. It is unfeasible in the present to make use of terminology that antedates the Code; such a practice, not uncommon among canonical writers, tends to generate confusion. Where the legislator has defined, the definitions advanced by legalists are by comparison amateurish and undesirable. In the matter of delegation the Code has afforded a description, if not a definition. In the present chapter the words of the legislator will be proposed and elucidated.

Article I—Preliminary Notions

Before all else, there are certain concepts, fundamental in themselves, the exposition of which will be of distinct advantage for the comprehension of what is to follow. A brief consideration of these will lead logically to the specific theme of this work.

§1. *The Notion of Power*

The canons that treat of the principles of delegation are contained in the fifth title of the second book of the Code, which is inscribed, *De potestate ordinaria et delegata.* It is notable that, whereas the canons contained therein treat almost exclusively of the power of jurisdiction, the title was so framed as to be most ample. The term *potestas* is indeed so broad and extensive, that its specific meaning must be determined in each case from the context. It is derived from the Latin *posse*, meaning *to be able*, and in its native signification denotes merely an ability or capability of acting.

The context in which the term is found in the present study, is the second book of the Code, which treats of ecclesiastical persons. Since persons of their nature are free and moral agents, the context adds the element of morality to the generic notion of ability to do something. Power, therefore, here signifies a *moral faculty of doing, exacting or possessing something.* This notion in turn corresponds to the notion of *right* (*ius*) in the *subjective* sense;[1] thus it is distinguished from *right* in the *objective* sense, which is nothing more than law considered as an objective entity. Since power is, then, in the present context a moral faculty and a right, and not an unmoral potentiality, as electricity or gravitation, it is moreover rational and inviolable, and it imposes correlatively on others a true obligation not to impede the efficacious exercise of the same.[2]

Ecclesiastical power, in the sense exposed, may be divided into the power of orders and the power of jurisdiction. The power of orders is that power which refers directly to the sanctification of souls through the exercise of public divine cult and the confection and administration of sacraments and sacramentals.[3] The power of orders receives specific treatment where the Code speaks of the hierarchy,[4] and of the sacraments and sacramentals.[5] Only incidentally in the title now under discussion is such a power introduced, since Canon 210 determines that the power of orders is not subject to the general rules of delegation set forth in preceding canons.

§2. *The Notion of Jurisdiction*

The power of jurisdiction constitutes the primary matter about which delegation revolves; it is precisely this power

[1] Cappello, *Summa Juris Publici*, p. 10; Chelodi, *Jus de Personis*, p. 4.

[2] Chelodi, *Jus de Personis*, p. 4.

[3] Wernz, II, n. 3; Cappello, *op. cit.*, p. 183; Maroto, *Institutiones*, I, 567.

[4] Cf. can. 108 ss.

[5] Liber III, *De Rebus*, Pars I.

which in practice is constantly transmitted from one to another. The term *jurisdiction* derives from the Latin *ius dicere.* In Roman Law the meaning of this expression was restricted to the concept of judicial power.[6] In ecclesiastical law, however, jurisdiction implied the fullness of power—the power to legislate, to execute law even by coactive means, and to pass judgment on the controverted rights of ecclesiastical society and individuals.[7] This extensive sense of the term is not new, but has been in force since the times of Gregory the Great,[8] though occasionally the use of the restricted meaning has found its way into the sources.[9] The Code has seized upon the extensive meaning of the term, denoting the most ample power of government in all its functions.[10] In order that this intention of the legislator might be manifest, it is called *potestas iurisdictionis seu regiminis;*[11] the particle *seu* denotes the identity of concept, while the term *regimen* is explicative of the preceding word and reveals its extension.

Jurisdiction may, then, be defined as a *public power of ruling or governing others.*[12] If, however, the definition is to be restricted to the ecclesiastical forum, it may be described as a *public power granted by Christ or by His Church through a canonical mission, of governing the baptized to the end of eternal life.*[13] Concerning this definition the following may be noted:

a. It is called a *public* power to distinguish it from the mere economic or dominative power that is exercised by a husband over his wife, a father over his children, or a teacher over his pupils.[14]

b. This power is conferred directly by Christ, when it is question of the jurisdiction of the Church, as such, or of the Supreme Pontiff as successor of Peter, on whom Christ bestowed

---

6 Maroto, *Institutiones,* I, 660.

7 Pihring, lib. I, tit. XXXI, n. 1; Reiffenstuel, lib. I, tit. XXIX, n. 2 ss.

8 Wernz, II, n. 3, not. 19; Badii, *Institutiones,* p. 127, not. 1.

9 C. 16, X, *de majoritate et obedientia,* I, 33; c. un., *de foro competenti,* II, 2 in Clem.

10 Roberti, *De Processibus,* I, n. 38.

11 Can. 196.

12 Pihring, lib. I, tit. XXXI, n. 1.

13 Chelodi, *Jus de Personis,* p. 201; Cocchi, *Commentarium,* II, 218; Maroto, *Institutiones,* I, 661; Blat, *Commentarium,* II, 165.

14 Reiffenstuel, lib. I, tit. XXIX, n. 5.

the fullness of power. It is said to be conferred by the Church through a canonical mission when inferiors of the Supreme Successor of Peter *derive* from the Vicar of Christ a share in the power committed by Christ.

c. This power is exercised directly over the *baptized* alone, since only by baptism does one become a subject of the spiritual kingdom, according to the words of the Apostle, "What have I to do to judge them that are without?" [15]

d. *Eternal life* is the ultimate end of ecclesiastical society, which is attained directly by the sanctification of souls.

That the power of jurisdiction, understood in the above sense, exists in the church, is asserted by the legislator.[16] It is, moreover, a matter of faith, as appears from the Encyclical of Pius IX, *Etsi Multa*,[17] the Constitution of Pius VI, *Auctorem Fidei*,[18] in which the second proposition of the *Synodus Pistoriensis* was condemned, and from the encyclical of Pius X, *Pascendi*.[19]

§3. *Non-Jurisdictional Powers*

The principles of delegation contained in the Code must be applied to the exercise of the power of jurisdiction. There are, however, other forms of power to be encountered which to some degree at least must be apt matter for delegation, though the legislator has not considered them directly in the title of which this paper treats. A brief consideration of these powers will not be foreign to the present study.

The Code states that the superiors of a clerical exempt religion enjoy ecclesiastical jurisdiction over their subjects, while certain other superiors have only a *dominative power* (*potestatem habent dominativam*).[20] St. Thomas [21] refers to dominative power as that which masters obtain over their slaves; and he distinguishes this from the *paternal* (*patria*) power which parents exercise over their children, and from the *economic* (*oeconomica*) power which regulates the subordination of wives

---

[15] I Cor. V, 12; cf. can. 12; 87.
[16] Can. 196.
[17] Ep. encycl. *Etsi Multa*, Nov. 21, 1873—Fontes, n. 566.
[18] Aug. 28, 1794—Fontes, n. 475.
[19] Sept. 8, 1907—Fontes, n. 680.
[20] Can. 501, §1.
[21] Summa, II, II, q. 57, art. 4; II, II, q. 104, art. 5 ad I.

to their husbands. These various distinctions of power in modern literature have been fused into one generic term, *dominative power.*[22]

Dominative power is quite distinct from true jurisdiction. St. Thomas [23] explained its scope by the phrase, "Domini est solummodo praecipere de agendis." It is an attribute of an imperfect society, which may be incapable to possess in itself true jurisdiction. The possessor of such power cannot make laws, exercise judgments or inflict serious penalties; he may, however, give precepts and punish the infringement of the same by milder penalties.[24] In religion this power is acquired by the superiors only when by profession the religious voluntarily subject themselves to the institute.[25]

If, then, dominative power is to be accepted as specifically that power which religious superiors, who enjoy no jurisdiction, exercise over their professed religious, it becomes necessary to inquire for other forms of power which are neither dominative nor jurisdictional. Novices, since they have not yet professed themselves, cannot be subject to the dominative power of their Master, because such power is acquired only by profession. The Code, however, does not mention a distinct power which might be asserted to apply to the novice. Biederlack-Führich [26] state that the legislator presupposes such a power, since from the very law of nature a certain degree of power accrues to the superior of every unified group that tends by common means towards a common end. Such a power may be termed *domestic,* or *social,* as Raus prefers.[27]

Hence, a third type of power must be admitted by which those who live a common life, are subjected to a superior in those things which make for a natural unity and order in the community. Thus novices are bound by such a power and even secular priests living a community life without any vows, as in a house of studies.[28] By virtue of this power the superiors are competent to oblige their subjects to those acts that are postu-

---

[22] Maroto, *Institutiones,* I, 662.
[23] II, II, q. 108, art. 5, ad III.
[24] Wernz, III, n. 689.
[25] Raus, *De Sacrae Obedientiae Virtute et Voto,* p. 65.
[26] *De Religiosis,* n. 36.
[27] *De Sacrae Obedientiae Virtute et Voto,* p. 115.
[28] Pesch, *Praelectiones Dogmaticae,* IX, n. 253.

lated by good domestic order. It is in this sense that the Code has determined that the novice is subject to the power of the Master and of the Superiors of the religion and that he is obliged to obey them.[29] When the novice makes profession, the domestic power of the Superiors is, as it were, absorbed by the dominative power newly acquired.[30] It is to be noted, however, that in clerical exempt religious the novices will be subject to the jurisdictional power of the legitimate superiors.[31]

Suarez [32] acknowledges in a religious prelate a threefold power, among which he mentions the power which arises from a vow (*potestas ex voto*). Whenever a vow of obedience is pronounced, an obligation from the virtue of religion arises. Hence, a power, correlative to this obligation, is quite conceivable as an entity distinct from either the power of jurisdiction or dominion. The superior enjoys the right to issue a precept, through the medium of which an actual and specific obligation arising from the vow becomes imminent. Suarez [33] regards as a mere play on words the contention that in such a case the Superior has no real power, but merely places a condition (the precept), on which the actual urgency of the vow depends. The result of his precept is always such that the person bound by the vow must obey as a matter of conscience. The power arising from the vow is, therefore, a special title by reason of which a Superior may oblige his subject.[34] The Superior is in quasi-possession of the right which corresponds to the obligation of the person bound by vow. Since the vow was necessarily made to God, the Superior in exercising this right does so by a vicarious power in the name of God.[35]

The Code seems to make explicit mention of the power arising from a vow when it states that a religious, passing over to another institute and thus repeating his novitiate, is bound to obey the Novice-Master and the Superiors of the new institute also by reason of his vow of obedience (*etiam ratione voti oboe-*

[29] Can. 561, §2.
[30] Vermeersch-Creusen, *Epitome*, I, n. 574.
[31] Raus, *De Sacrae Obedientiae Virtute et Voto*, p. 126.
[32] Tr. VII, l. X, c. 8, n. 1.
[33] Tr. VIII, 1. II, c. 8, n. 2.
[34] Raus, *De Sacrae Obedientiae Virtute et Voto*, p. 92.
[35] Raus, *De Sacrae Obedientiae Virtute et Voto*, p. 104.

dientiae).[36] Since the new religion does not acquire true dominative power over the religious until he is again professed, it is to be concluded that such a religious is bound to obey the Superiors by reason of their domestic or social power, by reason of their jurisdiction, if it is a clerical exempt religion, and also (*etiam*) by reason of the vow of obedience, if such has already been pronounced in the former institute.

§4. *The Extent of the Title on Ordinary and Delegated Power*

The fifth title of the second book of the Code has been inscribed, as was noted above, *De potestate ordinaria et delegata.* In the preceding pages mention has been made of several distinct types of ecclesiastical power. Do the canons of the present title apply to all these forms of power?

It has already been asserted that the Code is not concerned with domestic or social power, but rather presupposes it. The power arising from a vow is mentioned with regard to the religious who repeats a novitiate in another institute. Far more important, then, are the powers of jurisdiction and of dominion. It appears that the canons of this title are applicable to at least these last two forms of power. While the canons refer only to jurisdiction, the title is not inscribed *de iurisdictione ordinaria et delegata.* It is not enough to say that the title was constructed in a broad manner in order to include the last canon on the power of orders; this canon could very well have been added to the more restrictive title since it merely asserts in substance that the norms set forth in the preceding canons with regard to the delegation of jurisdiction are not to be applied to the power of orders. Hence, the title employed by the legislator excludes, rather than includes, the power of orders.

Creusen[37] contends that the rubric is to be understood only as referring to the power of jurisdiction and of orders. He does extend, however, the same principles to dominative power by virtue of Canon 20, which provides that in the event of the lack of an express provision of law, a norm is to be assumed from other laws made for similar matters and from general principles of law. Creusen applies the principles to both forms of power because of the analogy existing between them.

---

[36] Can. 633, §1.

[37] Vermeersch-Creusen, *Epitome,* I, n. 274.

Maroto,[38] on the other hand, regards the inscription of this title as a valid argument to prove that the principles contained therein are applicable to all powers that are similar to jurisdiction, such as economic and dominative power, and the like.

Practically, despite this minor controversy, it is certain that the principles of delegation as contained in the Code are applicable, whether directly or by force of reflex principles, to dominative power, to the power to assist at marriages [39] and similar powers.

Article II—The Definition of Delegated Power

Jurisdiction may be divided, by reason of the title by which it is acquired, into ordinary and delegated jurisdiction. The Code has described both in these simple terms:

Can. 197, §1. **Potestas iurisdictionis ordinaria ea est quae ipso iure adnexa est officio; delegata quae commissa est personae.**

§1. *Ordinary Jurisdiction*

Ordinary jurisdiction is that which is attached to an office by the law itself. This definition is not new. In Roman law it is stated that he who enjoys jurisdiction in his own right, and not by virtue of another's benevolence, may delegate it; [40] to enjoy power in one's own right was to have it from an office properly possessed. Reiffenstuel [41] describes it as that "which by law, canon or custom, belongs to someone in his own right, or by reason of his office or dignity." Pihring [42] and Schmalzgrueber [43] offer similar descriptions. In the definition of the Code two elements are conspicuous; (a) the power must be attached to an ecclesiastical office; and (b) the connection between power and office must be effected by disposition of the law itself (*ipso iure*). In general it might be stated that the

[38] *Institutiones*, I, n. 694.

[39] Pont. Comm. ad CC. Auth. Interp., 28 Dec. 1927—*AAS*, XX (1928), 61.

[40] Fr. 5, D. 2, 1.

[41] Lib. I, tit. XXIX, n. 11.

[42] Lib. I, tit. XXXI, n. 4.

[43] Lib. I, tit. XXXII, n. 5.

older authors insisted more on the first element than on the second.[44]

The first requisite of ordinary power is that it be attached to an ecclesiastical office. The Code thus defines an office in the strict sense:

> Est munus ordinatione sive divina sive ecclesiastica stabiliter constitutum ad normam sacrorum canonum conferendum, aliquam saltem secumferens participationem ecclesiasticae potestatis sive ordinis sive iurisdictionis. (Can. 145, §1.)

Such an office is distinguished from an office accepted in the broad sense, which is any duty legally exercised unto a spiritual end. Thus the offices of sacristan, choir-master, secretary to a bishop, and the like, are offices only in the broad sense. In the Code, unless the contrary is made manifest by the context, the term *officium* must be accepted in the strict sense.[45] Hence, where the legislator defines ordinary power as that attached to an office, the strict meaning of the term logically must be applied.

De Smet,[46] while he accepts the conclusion of the authors who require that the office be understood in the strict sense, protests that he is not convinced. He feels that since the term *officium* is contraposed to *persona* in the definition of ordinary and delegated power, any office, whether in the broad or strict sense, will suffice that power attached thereto be ordinary, since thus the contraposition continues to be sustained. Vlaming,[47] too, adheres to this opinion, since he maintains that the faculties of simple priests and confessors to dispense from certain matrimonial impediments are ordinary powers, thus receding from the contrary opinion which he professed in the text of his book.[48] This author[49] explains that the faculties in question, when granted to pastors by the Code, are ordinary, because they are annexed to an office taken in the *strict* sense; when granted

---

[44] Hilling, "Begriff und Umfang der potestas jurisdictionis ordinaria und delegata nach geltendem Kirchenrecht," *AkKR*, CIV (1924), 181-205.

[45] Can. 145, §2.

[46] *De Sponsalibus et Matrimonio*, n. 799, not. 3.

[47] *Praelectiones Juris Matrimonii*, II, 393.

[48] *Op. cit.*, n. 415.

[49] *Op. cit.*, II, p. 393, not. 4.

to the priest or confessor, they are ordinary since they are attached to an office accepted in the *broad* sense. To this same opinion Farrugia [50] seems to accede, since he regards the faculties mentioned above as ordinary.

The opinion of these authors is not acceptable. The Code prescribes in general that the term *officium* be understood in the strict sense.[51] De Smet weakly contends that the context seems to suggest (*innui videtur*) the contrary.[52] So mild a suggestion is not sufficient to undermine the positive presumption established by the Code, by which an office is presumed to signify a strict ecclesiastical office.

Furthermore, if an office accepted in the broad sense is a sufficient basis for ordinary power, the following incongruities must follow:

a. Canon 883 prescribes that confessors approved by their own Ordinary, or by the Ordinary of the port of embarkation or of any intermediate port, may, not only while they are traveling at sea, but also while they visit at intermediate ports, absolve their fellow-travellers, and even the faithful of the said intermediate ports, from cases reserved even to the Ordinary. Since the confessor possesses an office taken in the broad sense, and since the Ordinary who has approved him is incompetent to delegate him for such effects, it is to be concluded that his power is annexed by law to his office. His power, then, according to the opinion of the authors quoted above, ought to be ordinary. This, however, is not the case. Canon 873 determines who enjoy ordinary penitential jurisdiction, and the approved confessor travelling at sea is not enumerated there. The power, then, is not ordinary, precisely because it is attached to an office accepted in the broad sense.

b. All priests may validly absolve any rightly disposed penitent from all sins and censures, when the latter is found in the danger of death.[53] If the dispensing power of a mere priest is ordinary inasmuch as it is attached to an office accepted in the broad sense, then too this power to absolve in danger of death must be ordinary and for the same reason. This, however, is

---

[50] *De Matrimonio,* n. 86.
[51] Can. 145, §2.
[52] *Op. cit.*, n. 799, not. 3.
[53] Can. 882.

repugnant, for no one may maintain that all priests are ordinary confessors for those in danger of death. Such are not enumerated in Canon 873.

De Smet [54] goes further and questions whether, after all, a confessor does not enjoy a strict office. There is no probability to this. If such were the case, then surely the confessor traveling at sea, and the simple priest of Canon 882, who becomes a confessor *ipso iure* when he attends a person placed in danger of death, would be ordinary confessors, since the law itself attributes certain powers to their office. The only reason conceivable why they are not ordinary confessors, is precisely because their office is not a fit basis for ordinary power.

Finally, it is impossible to conceive a simple priest as the participant of ordinary power, as the authors cited above would have one believe. The priesthood is not an office but a state. Ordination does not confer an office,[55] but imprints a character which cannot be lost. Ecclesiastical offices, however, can be lost for various causes.[56] An office must, therefore, be regarded as something quite distinct from the priesthood. Indeed, many authors contend that an ecclesiastical office postulates a share in ordinary power.[57] If this is true, it is quite manifest that the priesthood is not such an office.

The office, therefore, which is the basis for ordinary power must be an office accepted in the strict sense of the Code. It must, consequently, be a sacred function established by divine or ecclesiastical authority; no civil power is competent to institute such an office. It must, moreover, be constituted permanently (*stabiliter constitutum*). The permanency of an office may be conceived in two ways. First, the office may be permanent in the sense that the incumbent thereof enjoys a perpetual title to the same, and thus cannot be deprived of it except in the specific manner and for the specific reasons described by the law; this is called *subjective* perpetuity. Secondly, an office may be perpetual in the sense that once established it becomes a juridical entity of itself perpetual, in such a way that, should the actual incumbent cease to be such, the office remains and

[54] *De Sponsalibus et Matrimonio*, n. 799, not. 3.

[55] Wernz-Vidal, *Jus Canonicum*, II, 164.

[56] Can. 183, §1.

[57] Wernz-Vidal, *op. cit.*, II, 165; De Meester, *Compendium*, I, n. 394; Chelodi, *Jus de Personis*, n. 131; Badii, *Institutiones*, n. 126.

postulates a successor; this is termed *objective* perpetuity, and it excludes all temporary functions that do not participate in the stability of common law. This objective perpetuity is required and suffices in order that an office might be regarded as an ecclesiastical office taken in the strict sense, to which ordinary power may be attached.[58]

Thus far only the first element essential for ordinary power has been considered. The second essential element consists in the fact that the power must be attached to the office by the law itself (*ipso iure*). The law which so disposes may be general or particular; moreover, it may be written or unwritten (custom), as the older authors likewise admitted.[59] Thus, the ordinary power to dispense from the law of superiors was acquired by custom;[60] and the Code[61] now expressly concedes to bishops the power of dispensing from the laws of provincial Councils.[62]

The connection between office and power may be effected by a privilege accepted in the broad sense. Such a privilege is truly a law which is enacted in favor of some particular class of persons and which contains a favorable exception to the general law. Thus, among the privileges of Cardinals is mentioned their faculty to hear confessions throughout the entire world.[63] Cardinals, however, enjoy *ordinary* penitential jurisdiction.[64] Hence, power annexed to an office by force of a privilege in the broad sense is ordinary. This is not true, however, of a strict privilege, since it is merely a private law, which is no law at all, since laws are made for the common good.[65]

A power may well be conceived as annexed to an office by the law itself, if by disposition of law, *antecedently* to the persons to whom the office is conceded, such power is identified with the office. Thus the office and the corresponding power are conceived as independent entirely of the incumbent of the office;

---

[58] Maroto, *Institutiones*, I, 675; 831; Vermeersch-Creusen, *Epitome*, I, n. 227; Blat, *Commentarium*, II, 158; Golden, *Parochial Benefices in the New Code*, p. 4.

[59] Reiffenstuel, lib. I, tit. XXIX, n. 11; cf. c. 13, X, *de foro competenti*, II, 2.

[60] Wernz, I, 122.

[61] Can. 291, §2.

[62] Cocchi, *Commentarium*, II, n. 118.

[63] Can. 239, §1, n. 1.

[64] Can. 873, §1.

[65] C. 3, D. III; Maroto, *Institutiones*, I, 339 ss.

and just as the office is permanent, the power attached thereto is regarded quite as stable.[66]

Finally it may be said that a power may be ordinary, even if it does not pertain to the office to which it is attached from the very nature of that office. In other words, the power in question need not be essential to the office. It is enough that the power be attached to the office either extrinsically or intrinsically by the law itself. Concerning this more will be said where it is question of the existence of delegation *a iure* in the Code.

§2. *Proper and Vicarious Jurisdiction*

An authentic division of ordinary power is contained in the Code in these terms:

***Can. 197,* §2. Potestas ordinaria potest esse sive propria sive vicaria.**

The legislator has been silent concerning the nature of proper and vicarious power; he reveals nothing more than the fact that both are ordinary. Before the Code the nature of the power of Vicars was the object of keen dispute.[67] Santi [68] regarded their power as a fusion of ordinary and delegated power. Wernz [69] inclined to the opinion that their power was more similar to delegation. Many regarded it as a power entirely distinct from either division of power.[70] This entire dispute has been ended by the practical decision of the legislator in the Code.

Both proper and vicarious power enjoy a common element: they are both ordinary—attached to an office by the law itself. They differ in the fact that he who enjoys proper power, acts in his own name, while he who enjoys vicarious power, acts in the name of him whose vicar he is. In this the vicar resembles the delegate who likewise acts in the name of another; the delegate, however, does not act by virtue of a power attached by law to his office, and in this he differs from the vicar. Hence,

[66] Wernz-Vidal, *Jus Canonicum,* II, n. 366.

[67] Cf. above, p. 26.

[68] Lib. I, tit. XXVIII, n. 21.

[69] II, n. 545.

[70] Hilling, "Begriff und Umfang der potestas jurisdictionis ordinaria und delegata nach geltendem Kirchenrecht," *AkKR,* CIV (1924), 183.

vicarious power, while it is ordinary, bears resemblance to delegated power. This fact has caused Prümmer [71] to state that all delegated power is vicarious. This is no longer a happy expression, since the Code has clearly opposed vicarious and delegated power to each other. No delegated power is vicarious, if the terms are employed, as is fitting, in the sense they enjoy in the Code.

Reiffenstuel [72] placed the distinction between vicar and delegate in the *place* where each exercises his power. If the power was exercised in the same place or tribunal wherein the Ordinary was wont to preside, the power was vicarious; if it was exercised elsewhere, it was delegated. This distinction is no longer valid. In the Code the sole distinction between the two must be placed in the fact that vicarious power, since it is ordinary, is attached by law to the office, while delegated power is entrusted to a person. The element of place does not enter into the matter.

The two terms, proper and vicarious power, are sometimes applied in a broader sense to the universal power of the Church. In this sense, that power is proper which naturally flows from the condition of the Church as a perfect society, and the Pope, dispensing from an ecclesiastical law, is said to use proper power. On the other hand, that power is vicarious which the Pope uses, acting as the Vicar of Christ, dispensing from vows and oaths, dissolving unconsummated marriages, and the like.[73]

§3. *Delegated Jurisdiction*

Delegated power might be described simply as *that which is not ordinary*. It is for this reason that a lengthy discussion of ordinary power has been submitted in the preceding pages. If power fails to verify any of the elements required for ordinary power, it is not ordinary but delegated. The Code has defined delegated power as *that which is committed to a person* (*quae commissa est personae*). It has thus established an adequate division of all power into ordinary and delegated power, so that every power that is not the one, must be the other. The two categories are, therefore, mutually exclusive. All other divisions

[71] *Manuale*, Q. 86.
[72] Lib. I, tit. XXVIII, n. 17.
[73] Wernz-Vidal, *op. cit.*, II, 359.

of jurisdiction, by reason of whatsoever title, such as forum, origin or extension, can be reduced to this prime distinction, so that all power, universal or particular, contentious or voluntary, is at the same time ordinary or delegated. Since delegated power is that which is committed to a person, delegation is the act of committing to another a power fit to be transmitted.

The concise definition of the Code merely presents in admirable form the definitions of the old authors. Reiffenstuel [74] defines delegated power as "that which one does not possess in his own right, but only by the commission of another, whose place he fills." Pihring [75] offers about the same, though his definition embraces both delegation and subdelegation. Schmalzgrueber,[76] as well as Pihring, makes clear in his definition the possibility of delegation *a iure*. Wernz [77] describes it as a concession of jurisdiction to be exercised in the name, and in the right, of another by force of a commission. All these descriptions conform to the natural signification of the term; [78] it is merely the substitution of another in the exercise of one's own power.

It is to be noted that delegated power is derived power; but not all derived power is delegated. All power in the Church is ultimately derived from Christ; hence, the ordinary power of the Roman Pontiff is at the same time derived. Similarly, other prelates are said to derive their power immediately from the Vicar of Christ, though at the same time their power may be ordinary, not delegated.[79]

In delegation a twofold person is to be considered; the one who enjoys a power that is according to the norms of law delegable, is the *delegator;* the one who is legally fit to receive and to exercise this power is the *delegate.* The first is the source of the power enjoyed by the second; he cannot give more than he possesses. The power of the delegate is not properly his own, but that of the delegator; hence, if the latter enjoys Papal or

---

[74] Lib. I, tit. XXIX, n. 12.

[75] Lib. I, tit. XXXI, n. 1.

[76] Lib. I, tit. XXXII, n. 5.

[77] II, n. 557.

[78] Forcellini-Perin, *Lexicon* v. *Delego:* "Delego est: aliquem mitto, ut meo nomine aliquid agat; adeoque demando, committo, trado alteri, qui meas vices impleat."

[79] Wernz-Vidal, *Jus Canonicum,* II, n. 368.

episcopal power, the power transmitted will be by nature Papal or episcopal power. It is the person of the delegate that constitutes the differentiating note between ordinary and delegated power; without him delegated power cannot be conceived. On the contrary, ordinary power may well be conceived without an actual incumbent in possession of the office to which it is attached; it is conceived as adhering to the office. Consequently, the definition of the Code (*commissa personae*) most accurately supplies the fundamental concept of delegated power.

§4. *Subdelegation*

Not only ordinary power may be regarded as delegable, but delegated power, too, may be committed to others within the restrictions established by law. When the power committed to another is not ordinary, possessed by virtue of an office to which the law has attached it, but delegated, that is, possessed by virtue of a commission made by the possessor of ordinary power, it is said to be subdelegated. This term merely denotes reiterated delegation. It is *mediate* delegation, proceeding from the ordinary officer to the subdelegate through the medium of a delegate. The concept, therefore, of delegation and subdelegation is fundamentally identical; it is the commission of power to a person. The total difference lies in the person of the delegator or subdelegator, as the case may be. The delegator enjoys ordinary power and transmits it to a delegate; the subdelegator enjoys delegated power and transmits it to a subdelegate.

Article III—Divisions of Delegation

The Code does not provide a series of specific types of delegation. To do so is the scope of commentators. The first division of delegation into immediate and mediate delegation or subdelegation has already been discussed. A few of the more important divisions may be proposed as follows:

a. Delegation may proceed from the *Apostolic See* or from an *inferior prelate*. The first was regarded as most noble in Roman law where ample powers were acknowledged in the *Delegatus a Principe*. The Code has extended this expression to include all who in law come under the name of Apostolic See.[80]

[80] Can. 7.

b. Delegation may be granted by reason of a *dignity* or *office;* or it may be granted simply by reason of the *person*. In the first case it is called *real* delegation; in the second, *personal.* It must be remembered that all delegation is personal, since it is committed to a person.[81] Hence, in real delegation the power is entrusted to the person, but by reason of his office. Such a delegation is regarded as passing from one incumbent of the office to another, yet always attributed to the person and not to the office. Maroto[82] regards as personal that delegation which is granted *electa industria personae.* It is not in this sense that Reiffenstuel[83] or, more recently, Vidal,[84] have understood personal delegation. Delegation, however, that is conceded *electa industria personae* might aptly be termed *strictly personal,* in order to distinguish it from the simple form of delegation that is conceded always to a person, but without any special consideration of the qualifications of that person.

c. Delegation may be *special* or *universal.* Special or particular delegation is that which is conceded for a particular case, or for several determined cases; universal delegation (*ad universitatem negotiorum*)[85] is that which extends to every species of power within the competence of the delegator, or at least to one determined class of affairs.[86] Thus, a priest delegated by a pastor to take full charge of parochial affairs during an absence, or a judge delegated for all matrimonial cases, would be a universal delegate.

d. Finally, delegation may be *ab homine* or *a iure.* This distinction was most frequent before the Code; the Code, however, does not employ it, unless with regard to censures.[87] Whether or not delegations arising from common law, without the intervention of a delegator, are contained in the Code, is an object of great dispute among canonists. To this question the chapter that follows will be devoted.

---

81 Can. 197, §1.

82 *Institutiones,* I, 844.

83 Lib. I, tit. XXIX, n. 39.

84 Wernz-Vidal, *op. cit.,* II, 361.

85 Can. 199, §3.

86 D'Annibale, *Summula Theologiae Moralis,* I, n. 71; Vermeersch-Creusen, *op. cit.,* I, n. 280.

87 Can. 2245, §2; 2252; 2253.

CHAPTER V

Some Controversies Related to the Notion of Delegation

Since delegation is a legal institute that is interwoven closely with the entire texture of law, the controversies in which it necessarily is involved, are without number. In the present chapter two major difficulties will be examined. These have been selected, not to depart from the scope of this work which is the general principles of delegation, and not specific problems, but because these questions are intimately related to the very concept of delegation. In a discussion of these problems much light may be cast on the fundamental notions that the preceding chapter has essayed to expose.

Article I—The Existence of Delegation *a Iure* in the Code

Delegation regularly proceeds from the person of a delegator to the person of the delegate. The source of delegation, however, need not be a physical person directly, but it may proceed from a disposition of law, in virtue of which the delegate acquires power. Such a delegation is called *a iure* to denote the source whence it proceeds. Under Tridentine legislation many were the cases in which Bishops acquired delegated power in this manner. The promulgation of the Code revealed the fact that the well known expressions of the old law had been omitted from the new. But what of the reality? Had it too disappeared, as did the terminology, or had it remained in the new law under the guise of other less patent phrases? Such questions have provoked various conflicting responses. The foremost opinions will be exposed briefly in the present article.

§*1. Total Exclusion of Delegation a Iure from the Code*

Immediately after the appearance of the Code Stutz[1] edited his work in which he maintained there was no longer need to

[1] *Der Geist des Codex Iuris Canonici*, p. 271.

retain the former distinction by which Bishops were said to act either as "Delegates of the Apostolic See," or "also as Delegates of the Apostolic See." [2] He contended that all such delegations had ceased to exist. In particular he pointed out the faculty of Ordinaries to dispense from certain irregularities arising from an occult crime,[3] the faculty to dispense from certain vows,[4] the faculty to permit bination,[5] the power to ordain outside the usual time,[6] and so forth. Stutz argued that all these faculties, and many others, which were formerly delegated faculties of Bishops, had become in the Code ordinary powers. His conclusion is that delegations *a iure* are entirely foreign to the Code.

The opinion expressed by Stutz cannot be accepted as entirely correct. There are certain delegations arising automatically from the law which must be reckoned with. Thus, every priest can absolve any penitent from all sins and censures in danger of death; [7] this power cannot be ordinary and is therefore delegated by common law. The same must be said of the priest who assists at a marriage according to the norm of Canon 1098, n. 2; he enjoys certain dispensatory powers that must be delegated by law. Similar examples can easily be multiplied.[8] Again, if all power is either ordinary or delegated, the supplied power of Canon 209 must be regarded as a delegation from the law. Then, the Apostolic Signatura sees certain matters by delegated power, as the Code explicitly asserts.[9] Finally, Canon 309, §4, provides for the singular case where the senior ecclesiastic, in point of service, must assume the reign of the Apostolic Vicariate or Prefecture when no other legally constituted administrator is available; the cleric thus succeeding acts as delegate of the Holy See.[10] Hilling [11] attempts to show that such an ecclesiastic would be an Ordinary. He argues that Canon 310 attributes to him the *ordinary* faculties of his prede-

[2] "Tamquam Sedis Apostolicae Delegati;" "etiam tamquam Sedis Apostolicae Delegati."

[3] Can. 990, §1.

[4] Can. 1313.

[5] Can. 806, §1.

[6] Can. 1006, §3.

[7] Can. 882.

[8] Cf. Can. 883; 990, §2, etc.

[9] Can. 1603, §2.

[10] ". . . censetur delegatus a Sancta Sede ut regimen assumat."

[11] *AkKR*, CIV (1924), 186.

cessor and that he, therefore, must be an Ordinary. However, Canon 310 merely states that he may *use* the ordinary faculties of his predecessor; that is, he as a delegate may make use of all the faculties which were ordinary to his predecessor. Hilling further urges that the same cleric is an Ordinary because he is one of those who succeeds in default of others, according to Canon 198, §1. This argument would be irrefutable, if Canon 309, §4, did not expressly state that the cleric in question is to be regarded as a delegate of the Holy See; the generic rule of Canon 198, §1, is derogated in the specific case now under discussion.

Hence, it must be said that at least some delegations arising from the common law yet exist in ecclesiastical legislation.

§2. *Frequent Presence of Delegation a Iure in the Code*

Fuster[12] and Ojetti[13] have assumed an attitude that is entirely at odds with that of Stutz. They maintain, in general, that all faculties conceded to Ordinaries by the Code that they might dispense from general laws of the Church, are delegated by the law. The basis of this opinion is a unique interpretation of Canon 197, §1, wherein ordinary power is described as that which is attached by law to an office. Ojetti states that this canon may be interpreted in one of two ways. First, in the sense that whatever is attributed to Ordinaries by the Code is by that very fact ordinary; or secondly, in the sense that only what is formally, or equivalently so, asserted in the Code to pertain to the nature of the office, is ordinary. The second interpretation, he maintains, is exclusively correct.

Ojetti profoundly inspects the notion of an ecclesiastical office and finds there are certain functions, without which such an office could not be conceived; such are essential to the office, so that if even one of these were taken away, the very office would be changed in nature. Thus, a Bishop's power to rule his diocese includes the legislative, judicial and coactive functions, all of which are essential to the office of bishopric. This

[12] "De la podestad ordinaria y delegada *a iure*," *Razon y Fe*, LXII (1921), 364 ss; LXIV (1923), 496 ss.

[13] "De Natura Potestatis Ordinariorum secundum Codicem," *Gregorianum*, VI (1925), 436–41.

office proceeds from a higher law than ecclesiastical law; the latter therefore must accept it according to the preformed concept of the legislator who created the office. Any elements superadded to this office as it existed according to this primitive concept are not essential, and consequently not ordinary.

A general reply to this contention might be summed up in the fact that the explanation is too labored and difficult. It is hard to believe that the legislator intended so to involve a matter that would admit of treatment far more facile. It is simple enough to determine the natural condition of an office according to the preformed idea of its creator when it is question of an office founded by divine right; it is most difficult, however, to do so when the office is of lesser institution. The legislator, indeed, defined in a simple manner the concept of ordinary power as that which is attached by law to the office; he did not introduce any distinction as to what was essential or non-essential. So long as a power is attached by law to the office it is ordinary. Where the legislator has not distinguished, it is not licit for canonists to do so. In fact, if the legislator wished to indicate that the power must pertain intrinsically to the office in order that it be ordinary, he might have chosen a happier expression than *adnexa officio;* such terms as *competere, cohaerere, adhaerere officio* would have more effectively indicated the need of a natural and essential bond between office and power. The words used in the Code rather indicate the contrary; the expression *adnexa officio* conveys the concept of *addition* to an office, which addition must be extrinsic to the office, since what is intrinsic is not conceived as additional but as constitutional.

Again, against the opinion of Ojetti and Fuster the following specific arguments are important:

a. Canon 912 states that, outside the Roman Pontiff, only they to whom it has been expressly conceded by law, can concede indulgences by force of *ordinary* power.[14] It is apparent, then, that there are some, other than the Pope, who may grant indulgences by their ordinary power. However, the granting of indulgences cannot be conceived as intrinsic and essential to any office inferior to the Papacy. St. Thomas[15] says, "The

[14] "Praeter Romanum Pontificem, cui totius spiritualis ecclesiae thesauri a Christo Domino commissa est dispensatio, ii tantum possunt potestate ordinaria indulgentias elargiri, quibus id expresse a iure concessum est."

[15] Quodlib. II, art. 16.

entire treasury lies in the dispensation of him who rules over the general Church; wherefore to Peter the Lord has committed the keys of the kingdom of heaven." In the same article he notes the requisites necessary to concede indulgences, the second of which is authority. He concludes, saying, "The Pope is able to grant indulgences principally; others only in so far as they have received from him the power, whether ordinary or committed, that is, delegated." Hence, all inferiors of the Pope who concede indulgences, do so in so far as they have received from the Pope the necessary faculty, which consequently is not essential to inferior ecclesiastical offices. It must, therefore, be concluded that ordinary power can be attached to an office by extrinsic addition. In this sense Lehmkuhl [16] regarded as ordinary the power of Bishops, Cardinals and Legates to grant certain indulgences. Blat [17] regards the distinction of ordinary and delegated power in this matter as merely analogous. This is not true, for the power to concede indulgences pertains to the power of jurisdiction and not to the power of orders.[18] Canon 912, stating that the law itself concedes to some the ordinary power of granting indulgences, by those very words makes it clear that ordinary power may be annexed to an office extrinsically.

b. Cappello [19] notes that Cardinals are *ordinary* confessors throughout the entire world. Yet such jurisdiction is by no means essential to the Cardinalatial dignity, but is counted among the privileges of that office.[20] It is, therefore, an extrinsic addition.

c. Faculties to dispense from general laws of the Church have long been regarded as ordinary. Thus, Gasparri [21] regarded as ordinary the faculty of bishops to dispense from matrimonial impediments, although such a power is not connatural to the episcopal office. To this opinion St. Alphonsus [22] agrees, while D'Annibale [23] calls it "most common." Wernz,[24] while holding

[16] *Theologia Moralis,* II, n. 536.
[17] *Commentarium,* III, n. 244.
[18] St. Thomas, *Suppl.,* q. xxvi, art. 2.
[19] *De Sacramentis,* III, n. 234.
[20] Can. 239, §1, n. 1.
[21] *De Matrimonio,* n. 404.
[22] *Theologia Moralis,* VI, n. 613.
[23] *Summula Theologiae Moralis,* I, n. 231.
[24] IV, n. 617, not. 63.

that the faculties granted to Ordinaries under date of February 20, 1888,[25] are not ordinary, but delegated, nevertheless maintains[26] that the power to dispense from impedient impediments established by common law is ordinary, even though such power had arisen from custom. The same author[27] likewise holds as ordinary many other faculties connected with matrimony, especially with regard to revalidation of marriages contracted defectively before the Church. Since, therefore, many powers possessed by inferior prelates over the general laws of the Church were regarded as ordinary before the Code, it is not clear why they should be regarded as less under the Code.[28]

d. The Code has amplified the notion of ordinary power which now includes vicarious power, formerly regarded as delegation or a unique form of power. Hence, under ordinary power must be included not only those powers which are essential to an office, but also those that are to be exercised by a vicar in virtue of his office, though in the name of another. It seems the evident intention of the Code to make ordinary the powers that authors previously had termed quasi-ordinary, mandated, and the like, all of which were regarded as very similar to ordinary power. Faculties, therefore, that do not pertain essentially to the nature of an office may very well be conceived as ordinary in the wider meaning of this term.

e. Ordinaries before the Code frequently acted as *Delegates of the Apostolic See.* This clause generally has been omitted in the Code. Such an omission can be regarded as nothing but intentional. Indeed, whenever the legislator wishes to specify the delegation of power, he makes specific mention of it, as in the case of the Apostolic Signatura,[29] synodal judges,[30] and the temporary administrator of the Prefecture or Vicariate Apostolic.[31]

f. Finally, Canon 1051 declares that the legitimation of natural offspring is effected by a dispensation from a diriment impediment granted either by ordinary power, or by power

[25] Fontes, n. 1109.
[26] IV, n. 615.
[27] IV, n. 618 ss.
[28] Vermeersch-Creusen, *Epitome,* I, n. 277.
[29] Can. 1103, §2.
[30] Can. 1574, §1.
[31] Can. 309, §4.

delegated through a general indult, but not indeed if the dispensation is granted by power delegated through a particular rescript. This canon, then, mentions power that is either ordinary, or delegated by a general indult, or delegated by particular rescript. There is no mention of a power delegated *a iure.* What, then, is the effect of a dispensation granted by a Bishop according to Canon 1043, which in the opinion of the adversaries would be a delegation from the law? No one will deny that such a dispensation is sufficient to produce legitimation. Therefore, the power of the Bishop in this case, since it is not delegated by general or particular indult, must be ordinary, if it is at all contained in Canon 1051.[32]

The proponents of the opinion, which has here been commented upon, have proposed one argument that demands special consideration. Canon 81 states that Ordinaries may not dispense from general laws of the Church, unless the power to do so has been conceded to them explicitly or implicitly. The reason for this is stated in the preceding canon which says that dispensations may be granted only by the legislator, his superior or successor, or by him to whom the same have conceded the faculty to dispense. Ojetti,[33] understands the last phrase to apply only to delegates, so that the sense of the canon would be that only the legislator, his superior or successor, or the *delegate,* of any of these, would be competent to dispense from a law. Since Bishops are not the legislators of general laws, nor superiors or successors of the legislators, the conclusion would be that they dispense in such laws as delegates.

This interpretation is not sound. The Code states that a dispensation may be granted *ab illo cui iidem (conditor legis, successor, superior) facultatem dispensandi concesserint.* It is to be noted that a concession does not imply necessarily a delegation. Every delegation is a concession; not every concession is a delegation. This power may be conceded in such a way as to be granted by law to an office, independently of the actual personal incumbent of the same. In such a case the power would be ordinary.

---

[32] O'Keeffe, *Matrimonial Dispensations,* p. 100.

[33] *Commentarium,* I, 328, not. 10.

This explanation is not without difficulties.[34] Canon 2253, n. 3, treating of a censure reserved in the law, states that those competent to absolve from the same are either he who has pronounced the censure or he to whom it is reserved, the successors or superiors of the same, or their delegates. Moreover, Canon 2237, §2, provides that Ordinaries in occult cases may absolve from censures reserved simply to the Holy See by common law. Now, in which member of Canon 2253, n. 3, is mention made of the Ordinary absolving in an occult case from a censure simply reserved by law to the Holy See? According to Fuster, such an Ordinary is not the inflicter of the censure, nor he to whom it is reserved, since it is reserved to the Holy See; nor is he the successor or competent superior of either of these. Consequently, it is contended, he must be the delegate. Therefore, an Ordinary absolving from such a censure established by common law does so, not by ordinary power, but in virtue of a delegation contained in the law itself.

In response to this difficulty it might be stated that even if Ordinaries absolved from certain censures in virtue of a delegation proceeding from the law, it would not, therefore, follow that they dispensed from general laws of the Church by delegated power. It would only prove that in absolving from censures, which is an entirely different matter from the concession of dispensations, Ordinaries proceeded as delegates of the Holy See.

However, this objection does not seem to be irrefutable. While Canon 2253, n. 3 makes explicit mention of the delegate, the more general Canon 2236, §1, avoids such a term and carries in its place the phrase, *cui haec potestas commissa est.* Canon 80 makes use of a phrase equally broad, so that it may embrace both delegates and ordinary officers. It is not clear why Canon 2253, n. 3 should be more restricted than these other canons.

Moreover, it may truthfully be maintained that Canon 2253, n. 3 does not present a complete enumeration of those who may absolve from censures reserved by law. Thus, Cardinals [35] may absolve from all censures, except those reserved in a most special manner to the Holy See and those inflicted for the vio-

---

[34] Fuster, "Sobre los delegaciones a iure en el nuevo Codigo," *Razon y Fe*, LXVI (1923), 499.

[35] Can. 239, §1, n. 1.

lation of the secret of the Holy Office. Cardinals, however, enjoy ordinary power.[36] Under what member, then, of Canon 2253, n. 3 could Cardinals be classified? They have not inflicted the censure; nor are they the successors or superiors of him who inflicted it; nor are they delegates, since their power is ordinary. Obviously, then, this canon makes no provision for Cardinals who absolve from a censure reserved by law to the Holy See. Again, the Penitentiary of Canon 401, §1 absolves by force of ordinary power from censures reserved by law to the Bishop. The adversaries will unsuccessfully attempt to classify this dignitary under the members of Canon 2253, n. 3. Hence, it must be concluded that the enumeration in that canon is demonstrative, not taxative. Therefore, the canon is not a valid proof that Ordinaries absolve from censures reserved to the Holy See by force of power delegated by the law.

§3. *Conclusion*

What opinion is most satisfactory in the controversy with regard to the existence of the delegations *a iure* in the Code? Creusen [37] replies: "We shall call ordinary every power conceded by law to one who holds a true office, v.g. Ordinaries, pastors, and so forth, unless the contrary is apparent in the text itself, as in Canon 1603, §2."

The opinion of Stutz is not entirely true. The opinion of Fuster and Ojetti is over subtle and gives rise to many difficulties that cannot be solved. If any doubt remains, it is necessary to return to the definition of ordinary power: *ea quae ipso iure adnexa est officio.*[38] This canon presumably is to be accepted according to the proper signification of the words.[39] The doubts generated in this question are not sufficient to necessitate departure from the simple definition of ordinary power. This is all the more true when such a departure creates in turn difficulties and doubts of a more serious character, and leads to an interpretation that is less favorable. In doubt, therefore, reflex principles will confirm the opinion quoted above in the words of Creusen.

[36] Can. 873, §1.

[37] Vermeersch-Creusen, *Epitome,* I, n. 277, 2.

[38] Can. 197, §1.

[39] Can. 18.

A practical conclusion of this discussion lies in the fact that all who enjoy an ecclesiastical office, properly accepted, may delegate others to exercise powers granted to them by the Code, such as the power to dispense from certain matrimonial impediments,[40] and from the law on the observance of feasts, fasts and abstinence.[41]

A final word might be added to this discussion with regard to the nature of these ordinary dispensatory powers granted by the Code to Bishops and others. Are they ordinary-proper or ordinary-vicarious? The concepts already presented in preceding pages can solve this difficulty.

Power is ordinary if it is attached by law to an office. There are, however, certain powers that are intimately and intrinsically connected with the office; while there may be others which are superadded to the office and which consequently can be detracted from the office without changing the nature of the same. This fact seems to be the basis for the distinction, made by the legislator, of proper and vicarious power.[42] Vicarious power is attached by law to the office; and by this fact it is truly ordinary. It differs, however, from proper (propria) power since it is exercised in the name of another, while proper power is exercised without regard to any other person. The vicar is, in a restricted sense, a secondary agent, making use of a power that pertains primarily to another.[43] At the same time, the vicar is not a delegate. Both act in the name of another, but the vicar's power has been acquired by the acquisition of an office, while the delegate has received power by force of a commission.

Consequently, to assert that the power of a Bishop to dispense from the law of his Superior is vicarious, does not imply a denial that it is ordinary but rather affirms it; hence, it implies a denial that it is delegated. It would appear, then, that a Bishop dispensing from a general law of the Church did so by vicarious power, since the act is placed in virtue of a power conceded by law to his office, in such a way that the power so conceded might be increased or extinguished entirely without

---

[40] Can. 1043 ss.

[41] Can. 1245, §1; cf. Haring, "Delegation pfarrlicher Dispensvollmachten," *LQS*, LXXIX (1926), 594-5.

[42] Can. 197, §2.

[43] Wernz-Vidal, *Jus Canonicum*, II, 359.

changing the nature of his office. Such a power is extrinsic, not connatural to the office; it is not a *potestas propria.*[44]

To admit that such dispensatory powers are vicarious should not be difficult for those who are inclined to the view that such faculties are perhaps delegated. As has been stated before,[45] the distinction between vicar and delegate in the old law was regarded as centered in the *place* where each exercised his jurisdiction; the vicar did so in the same place or tribunal as the Ordinary; the delegate did so elsewhere. In the new law the difference lies in the office to which the vicar's power is attached, while the delegate enjoys no strict office. Hence, it is no more repugnant to say that a Bishop, or even a pastor, acts as Vicar of the Holy See, than to assert that he does so as Delegate of the Holy See. Yet, before the Code, Bishops acted most frequently as Delegates of the Holy See. Therefore, it is quite congruous that they act after the promulgation of the Code as Vicars of the Holy See in those same and similar matters, if indeed such powers have been conceded to their office by the common law.

It would seem, then, that the power of Ordinaries to dispense from certain general laws in virtue of the disposition of the Code, is ordinary and vicarious. This opinion has won to itself, besides Maroto, already cited, such prominent canonists as Chelodi,[46] Cappello,[47] Cocchi,[48] Vidal,[49] Farrugia,[50] and De Smet.[51]

Creusen,[52] however, disagrees, maintaining that such faculties are ordinary, but proper. He states that before the Code such faculties were regarded simply as ordinary powers and that consequently they should be regarded as simply and properly ordinary in the new law. Furthermore, he is reluctant to grant that Bishops act in such matters in the name of the Holy See.

The latter objection does not cause great difficulty. In the present law, there is a striking juridical similarity existing

[44] Maroto, *Institutiones,* I, 829.

[45] Cf. p. 56.

[46] *Jus de Personis,* p. 202.

[47] *De Sacramentis,* III, n. 234.

[48] *Commentarium,* II, n. 118, c.

[49] Wernz-Vidal, *Jus Canonicum,* V, n. 411-413.

[50] *De Matrimonio,* n. 86.

[51] *De Sponsalibus et Matrimonio,* n. 755.

[52] Vermeersch-Creusen, *Epitome,* I, n. 277, 3.

between any vicar and a delegate, as was pointed out above. Since Bishops acted as Delegates in many cases then, it is not repugnant that they should act as Vicars now. Moreover, the correction of law is odious. It is, however, a lesser correction if delegated faculties become ordinary-vicarious than if they become ordinary-proper.[53] Nor does the first objection proposed by Creusen create much difficulty. This author quotes D'Annibale [54] as one who regarded such faculties as ordinary. D'Annibale, however, asserted this only with qualification, saying that Ordinaries dispensed in such matters *veluti iure ordinario.* The old authors in general were unwilling to assert without qualification that Ordinaries dispensed by force of a power that was strictly ordinary. For this reason they used such expressions as *quasi-ordinary or mandated power, veluti iure suo, quasi iure suo, etc.* By such expressions they manifested an intention of regarding these powers as something more than delegation, but something less than ordinary power, that was entirely proper to an office. The Code has extended the concept of ordinary power to include also vicarious power. It is reasonable, therefore, to embrace under this extension the powers that pre-Code writers regarded as very similar to ordinary power, though not identical with it.

Hilling,[55] agreeing with Creusen in this matter, proposes a distinct objection. In both the old and new law, as is evidenced in the case of the Vicar General, vicarious power is conceived as perishing whenever it is extinguished in the person who enjoys it principally. It is enough to recall, however, that the Official who is truly a Vicar in judicial matters, does not lose his power when the see becomes vacant, as the Code expressly states.[56]

In view of the foregoing considerations it is licit to conclude that the powers of an Ordinary, or of any one who enjoys a strict office, to dispense from general laws of the Church, if they are granted by law to the office, are ordinary-vicarious powers.[57]

---

[53] Maroto, *Institutiones,* I, 830, not. 1.

[54] *Summula Theologiae Moralis,* I, n. 231.

[55] *Loc. cit., AkKR,* CIV (1924), 195.

[56] Can. 1573, §5–§6.

[57] O'Keeffe too readily states that "all must admit" such faculties are not *ordinariae-propriae.* He erroneously believes that all the authors who regard them as ordinary, also hold them to be vicarious. Thus, for

Article II—The Nature of Power Granted to the Vicar General by Special Mandate

Before the Code it was not clear that a Vicar General enjoyed ordinary power; [58] the Code has made it manifest.[59] The Vicar General now possesses most ample jurisdiction, save in judicial matters. There are, however, many functions which he cannot perform without a special mandate.[60] When the Vicar has received from the Bishop a special mandate for a specific act, or series of acts, he becomes competent in those specific matters. In such a case, does he act by force of ordinary or delegated power?

Stutz,[61] Maroto,[62] and Vidal,[63] contend that such power is ordinary. On the other hand, Chelodi [64] maintains the contrary; to which Creusen [65] agrees, making light with Hilling [66] of the opinion of older writers who distinguished between those special mandates that were granted at the time a Vicar was nominated, and those given later and separately.

Those who contend that such power is ordinary, believe that the concession of a special mandate is merely determinative of the extent of the natural powers of the Vicar; furthermore, it is not given to a person, but to an office.

The opinion that regards such power as delegated, seems to be preferred. That power is ordinary which is annexed by law to an office. But the common law of the Church, which is the founder of the office in question, has effectively despoiled the office of certain functions. Therefore, instead of being attached by law to the office, these rights have been detached by law from the office. Hence, in order that the Vicar General be competent in such matters, he requires a mandate *ab homine*,

---

example, he cites Vermeersch-Creusen (*Epitome*, II, n. 307); but here these authors merely state that the power is ordinary. Elsewhere (I, n. 277, 3), entering the question professedly, they strongly contend them to be ordinary, but proper.—O'Keeffe, *Matrimonial Dispensations*, p. 95 ss.

[58] Wernz, II, n. 805.

[59] Can. 366.

[60] Cf. Can. 152; 455; 1104, etc.

[61] *Der Geist des Codex Juris Canonici*, p. 325.

[62] *Institutiones*, I, 830.

[63] Wernz-Vidal, *Jus Canonicum*, II, n. 640.

[64] *Jus de Personis*, p. 306.

[65] Vermeersch-Creusen, *Epitome*, I, n. 436, 3.

[66] "Die Jurisdiktion des Generalvikars," *AkKR*, CIV (1924), 204.

which is quite different from a disposition *a iure*.[67] Indeed, the legislator, by denying to the Vicar such powers, manifests his intention that regularly the functions in question should be under the intimate vigilance of the Bishop; such powers, then, are not to be regarded as proper to the office of Vicar.

Furthermore, it is not correct to assume that the extent of ordinary power attached to an office established by common law should be determined by one incapable of regulating common law. The authority that has established an office that bears with it a participation of power,[68] likewise establishes the extent of the power attached thereto. The office is an institution of common law, and only those powers granted by common law are ordinary.

It is to be noted that the phrase, *nisi ex mandato speciali,* is not added uselessly to the canons in which it appears. Were it not there, the canons would simply assert the incompetency of the Vicar General in such matters. Then, it might be doubted whether a Bishop could even delegate the Vicar for such matters, since the latter would have been declared incompetent by the law. The presence of the phrase makes it perfectly clear that delegation of the Vicar General is not prohibited.

Vidal[69] notes that by force of Canon 368, §1, Bishops may reserve to themselves certain acts which common law ascribes to the office of Vicar General. He argues that a Bishop so reserving to himself a particular function and later revoking the reservation, does not consequently by this revocation delegate the Vicar for the act, but rather amplifies the ordinary power of the Vicar. Similarly, he asserts, a special mandate merely amplifies the ordinary power and does not confer delegation.

The parity between these two cases is not sustained. It is the privilege of the Bishop to reserve certain acts to himself, which he enjoys by force of the same common law which has attributed such acts to the Vicar. He may effectively deprive the Vicar of certain rights which common law permits him. When he recalls this reservation, the rights and powers of the

---

[67] Toso, "Summa de officio et potestate Vicarii Generalis," *Jus Pont.*, VII (1927), 138-146; cf. n. 12.

[68] Can. 145, §1.

[69] *Jus Canonicum,* II, n. 640.

Vicar are restored to their normal condition, as expressed in the law. In other words, when a Bishop removes the reservation he has made, he does not grant any power at all, whether ordinary or delegated; he merely *removes an obstacle* which has prevented the office from possessing the amplitude of power conceded to it by law. On the other hand, by a special mandate he *confers powers* which the common law has effectively detached from the office of Vicar. In this case the Vicar, receiving the power, accepts something that is not attached by law to his office. It is, therefore, delegation.

CHAPTER VI

The Subject of Delegation

Delegation connotes a twofold person, the one who gives, the other who receives. It has already been suggested that power might accrue to the delegate from the law itself, without the apparent intervention of a delegator. But even in this case a delegator must be conceived, for the law which attributes power is ineffective in itself, unless behind the veil of legal terminology the legislator stands prepared to supply his authority. Delegation *a iure* is merely a legal fiction by which power, actually deriving from the legislator, is regarded as proceeding from common ecclesiastical law. Hence, in every act of delegation two ecclesiastical persons are involved. The person who gives of his power to another is the *active subject* of delegation; the person who receives, is the *passive subject* of delegation. They are so called since the relation between them is, philosophically, that of *agens* to *patiens*.

Article I—The Active Subject of Delegation

The active subject of delegation is the delegator. When he delegates, he elicits a human act. Hence, all that is required by the law of nature that an act be truly human, is demanded for the validity of the act of delegation. Consequently, that ignorance which is termed antecedent,[1] substantial error,[2] absolute violence,[3] and the like, vitiate the natural act by which power is committed to another. Grave fear does not naturally nullify the act, but by disposition of law an act placed under such fear unjustly inflicted, is rescindable at the will of the injured person.[4] Moreover, an act of delegation, not invalid by reason of natural defects, may be rendered null by positive law. In this

[1] Aertnys-Damen, *Theologia Moralis,* I, n. 27.
[2] Can. 104.
[3] Aertnys-Damen, *op. cit.,* I, n. 18; cf. Can. 103, §1.
[4] Can. 103, §3; cf. Maroto, *Institutiones,* I, n. 398.

manner, since to delegate is to exercise jurisdiction, an act placed by an excommunicated person after the pronouncement of sentence, whether condemnatory or merely declaratory, is quite valueless.[5] Similarly, a person suspended by condemnatory or declaratory sentence is incapable of delegating jurisdiction.[6] In a word, the act by which delegation is conferred, must be valid both naturally and juridically.

The Code has not determined in the title on ordinary and delegated power all the requisites demanded in the delegator that his acts might be valid. Many are determined by nature; many others the legislator has determined in specific legislation throughout the Code. In the present title, however, the law is most specific on the limits within which the delegator is free to commit to others his power. Since in law there is no place for infinity, taken indeed in the sense of a lack of limits, it was fitting that the lawmaker should determine accurately the demarcation between what would be valid, and what invalid, commission of power. Canon 199 indicates these limits, first by establishing the right to delegate; secondly, by determining the extension of the power to subdelegate.

§*1*. *The Right to Delegate*

Can. 199, §1. **Qui iurisdictionis potestatem habet ordinariam, potest eam alteri ex toto vel ex parte delegare, nisi aliud expresse iure caveatur.**

This principle was found in Roman law and at all times in the law of the Church. He who enjoys ordinary power, possesses it in his own right, by virtue of an office which he legitimately occupies. If power is at all delegable, he surely has the right to commit it to others, who possesses it in this manner. Hence, whoever enjoys ordinary power, whether it is proper or vicarious, may delegate it to another. Moreover, he may consign it to another in any measure or extent that he chooses (*ex toto vel ex parte*). He may commit, therefore, any part of his power, whether for one act, or for a species of acts; he may likewise delegate his entire power. This latter statement, however, must

[5] Can. 2264.

[6] Can. 2284.

be accepted only with qualification. An ordinary magistrate could not yield to another the plenitude of his power without restriction of time, reserving nothing to himself. Authors are generally agreed that to do this would be equivalent to abdication and to the designation of another ordinary, which cannot be done without the authority of the Supreme Superior.[7] To avoid this, some restriction must be imposed. This may be effected in several ways. The ordinary officer might commit his entire power to others in such a manner that no one delegate would enjoy the fullness of power; or he might commit his entire jurisdiction to one delegate for a limited period of time; or he might commit his entire power without restriction of time, but with definite restrictions as to the manner in which the power so delegated is to be exercised. In any of these fashions the intention not to abdicate is sufficiently established. Obviously, it is not desirable that the incumbent of an office should unburden himself of all, or nearly all, of his duties. Excessive and imprudent delegations will be illicit.[8]

The text now under discussion states that ordinary power can be delegated, unless the contrary is expressly provided for by law. Actually, the law has made certain express provisions to the contrary of the general rule of the canon. The Canon Penitentiary, who obtains ordinary jurisdiction to absolve from sins and censures, including even those reserved to the Ordinary, by express disposition of law is incapable of delegating his power to others.[9] Again, Cardinals, pastors and those who in law are equivalent to pastors, enjoy ordinary penitential jurisdiction.[10] In subsequent canons,[11] where the legislator has determined who may confer delegated confessional jurisdiction, there is no mention of Cardinals or those who come under the name of pastor. From this fact authors concluded that in the matter of jurisdiction for the confessional the Code had established an exception to the rule regarding the delegation of ordinary power.[12] With

---

[7] Wernz, II, n. 552; Reiffenstuel, lib. I, tit. XXIX, n. 56. Santi, lib. I, tit. xxix, n. 7; Vermeersch-Creusen, *Epitome,* I, n. 280, 1.

[8] C. 3, 28, X, *de officio et potestate iudicis delegati,* I, 29; Wernz, II, n. 552.

[9] Can. 401, §1.

[10] Can. 873, §1.

[11] Can. 874; 875.

[12] Maroto, *Institutiones,* I, 845, not. 2.

regard to Cardinals, this deduction becomes inassailable when one considers that the confessor chosen by a Cardinal for himself and his retinue acquires jurisdiction from the law itself, if he lacks it.[13] Were the Cardinal's power delegable, it would be sufficient that he invite a priest to hear the confessions of his entourage, without need of a special delegation *a iure* to render the priest competent. The Pontifical Commission for the Authentic Interpretation of the Canons of the Code on October 16, 1919, has made it manifest that those who in law come under the name of pastors, are unqualified to delegate their ordinary confessional jurisdiction.[14]

The power to assist at the celebration of a marriage is not properly jurisdictional; hence, the peculiar norms that regulate the delegation of such power, do not constitute strict exceptions to the present canon. Nevertheless, the act by which such power is conceded, is likened to the act by which a privilege, a faculty, or jurisdiction is conferred, as the Rota has declared.[15] Consequently, the Code [16] explicitly regards the faculty conceded in this matter as delegation. If, then, such power is accepted as quite similar to the delegation of jurisdiction, and to be governed by the same principles, another true exception to the canon now under discussion is stated in Canon 1096, §1. By virtue of this disposition, the ordinary assistant at marriages may not delegate his power wholly or in part to whomsoever he would. He may concede delegation to a determined priest for a determined marriage; and then only may he grant a general or universal delegation when the passive subject is truly a vicar cooperator, appointed according to the tenets of Canon 476.

Blat [17] has proposed another exception to the general rule of delegation. While he admits, against the opinion of Fuster and Ojetti, that the common faculties of Bishops to dispense from general laws are ordinary powers, not delegated, nevertheless he contends that such powers are not delegable; they come under the clause, *nisi aliud expresse iure caveatur.* The reason for this deduction is the fact that in certain canons it is explicitly stated

[13] Can. 239, §1, n. 1.

[14] *AAS*, XI (1919), 477.

[15] 20 Jan. 1911, *Casu Divionensi,—AAS*, III (1911), 284-293; cf. Benedict XIV, *Casus Conscientiae*, IV, 143.

[16] Can. 1096, §1.

[17] *Commentarium*, II, n. 148.

that the Ordinary may dispense either personally or through the medium of another (*per se vel per alium*); [18] but in many canons this explicit mention of the possibility of delegation is lacking.[19] Hence, he contends, unless one would say that the phrase *per se vel per alium* is quite useless wherever it appears, it is necessary to conclude that where it is present, delegation is possible; where it does not appear, delegation is prohibited.

A general response to the objection can be deduced from the canon now under discussion. This canon states that ordinary power may be delegated *unless the contrary is expressly provided for by law.* Hence, the general rule is to be presumed; the exception is to be proved. Blat, on the contrary, admitting that such faculties are ordinary, requires that in the matter of dispensation from a general law the application of the general rule be made *express.* In such an interpretation the canon should have stated that ordinary power may *not* be delegated, unless the contrary is expressly asserted by law. It will escape no one that such violence to Canon 199, §1, is repugnant. If this canon is to be accepted in its evident meaning, Canon 1043 and similar canons connote an ordinary power that is delegable, since no express provision to the contrary has been made.

It has been asserted that unless the interpretation of Blat is correct, the words *per se vel per alium,* wherever they appear, will be useless. However, one must remember that the explicit does not militate against the implicit. Hence, the fact that this clause is explicit in one case, by no means insinuates that the same liberty is not enjoyed in other cases where explicit mention of it is not made; in these latter cases, it is certainly contained implicitly, unless the contrary is stated in the law.[20] The clause is used in some cases merely unto abundance. This assertion can be proved from the Code where frequently the phrase is added in matters, concerning the delegability of which no one would have doubted, even had the words been omitted. And again, the phrase is lacking in canons, the powers of which no one will doubt to be delegable, despite the omission. If this is true, no argument can be drawn from the presence or absence

[18] Cf. v. g., can. 990, §1.
[19] Cf. can. 1028, §1; 1043; 1245; §1.
[20] Can. 199, §1.

of the phrase in a particular canon. It will be advantageous, then, to establish the truth of this contention in the following.

First, the phrase *per se vel per alium* is used by the Code in instances in which its omission would not have caused any doubt concerning the delegability of the powers mentioned therein. Canon 1397, §4, charges Ordinaries with the task of watching over the books that are published or sold in their territory, while Canon 1382 empowers them to visit all schools within their territory with regard to the moral and religious training imparted in the same. In both cases it is made explicit that the Ordinaries may execute these functions either personally or through others. Since, however, the Bishop is the natural guardian of faith and morals within his territory, who would deny that a Bishop could delegate to others matters that are essentially his own, even if explicit permission to delegate had not been granted? The power to delegate these acts of vigilance would have been perfectly clear, even had the phrase in question been omitted. Again, Canon 1443, §2, states that the Ordinary may delegate another cleric to effect the corporal institution of a person who has been granted a non-consistorial benefice. In this case, too, explicit mention of the power to delegate cannot be conceived as necessary. Likewise, Canon 1572, §1, decrees that the Ordinary is the judge in the first instance of all cases that are not reserved to a higher authority, and that he may exercise this power *per se vel per alios.* But even if this clause had not been added, no one would question the right of a Bishop to delegate the judgment of a case, when he enjoys ordinary jurisdiction in judicial matters from the very nature of his office.[21] Finally, religious profession must be made to the legitimate Superior or to his delegate,[22] while religious superiors are warned not to compel *per se aut per alium* their subjects to confess sacramentally to themselves.[23] In these and many other instances the explicit mention of the power to delegate has only made more clear what would have been undeniable, even had the Code been silent on the point.

On the other hand, there are canons of the Code in which explicit mention of the power to delegate is not found, though

[21] Can. 329, §1; 335, §1.
[22] Can. 571, §1, n. 6.
[23] Can. 518, §3.

no one may deny that such power is implicitly present. Thus, Canon 335, §1, declares the right of a Bishop to govern his diocese both in spiritual and temporal matters by means of the legislative, judiciary and coactive powers; it is not stated that he may do any of this by means of delegates, though it would be contrary to fundamental principles to deny it. Similarly, despite the omission of the use of a delegate in the prescriptions of Canon 464, §1, no one will deny this right to a pastor in exercising the care of the souls entrusted to him. The same may be said of Canon 468, §1, wherein is stated the sacred obligation of a pastor to care for the sick. Likewise, the judgment of cases involving certain privileged persons is reserved to the Roman Pontiff, who alone is competent; [24] here too, no mention is made of a delegate, though the use of distinguished clerics as delegates would be the normal procedure in such cases. Again, the Metropolitan is competent to see certain cases in which there is question of the temporal goods of a Suffragan; [25] though it is certain the Metropolitan may delegate this power, there is no explicit mention of delegation.

The instances presented above could be multiplied. Sufficient have been presented to make clear that nothing can be deduced from the presence or absence of explicit power to delegate. Wherefore, it is necessary to adhere to the general principle of Canon 199, §1, in virtue of which all ordinary power may be delegated. An exception in the matter of powers to dispense from general laws is, to say the least, not *express*, as the Code requires.

As a final word against the opinion now under discussion, it is well to call to mind that the power of Ordinaries to dispense from banns [26] is a power to dispense from a general law of the Church, for which no explicit permission to delegate is contained in the Code. Hence, according to the adversary, this power would not be delegable. This conclusion, however, would be contrary to a most general practice of the Church, since it is most common for bishops to delegate the power to dispense from one or more publications to rural deans, pastors, and other priests, and, indeed, without any special favor of the Holy See.

---

[24] Can. 1557, §1.
[25] Can. 274, n. 8; 1572, §2.
[26] Can. 1028, §1.

This point acquires more weight when it is recalled that the quinquennial faculties granted to Ordinaries may be delegated even habitually. In these faculties there is no special concession regarding dispensation from banns. Hence, if the power to dispense from banns were not delegable, the fact would be that Ordinaries could subdelegate their powers over impediments of a most serious character, and yet be unable to delegate in the less serious matter of dispensing from the proclamations.

§2. *The Right to Subdelegate*

Having established the power of ordinary magistrates to commit jurisdiction to their delegates, the legislator next considers the subsequent problem of subdelegation. In this matter the Code introduces a distinction between one delegated by the Apostolic See and the delegate of any inferior prelate. In the case of the delegate of any inferior prelate, a further distinction becomes necessary; one may be delegated universally, or for a particular matter. The Code treats of each of these possibilities in successive paragraphs, and concludes the canon by asserting the ultimate limit beyond which all further commission of power is invalid. These various principles will here be commented upon.

Can. 199, §2. **Etiam potestas iurisdictionis ab Apostolica Sede delegata subdelegari potest sive ad actum, sive etiam habitualiter, nisi electa fuerit industria personae aut subdelegatio prohibita.**

The first principle of subdelegation taken originally from Roman law, was acknowledged frequently in the Decretals. This privilege was always accorded to the delegate of the supreme authority, who was known technically as *Delegatus a Principe.*[27] Such a delegate, because of the dignity of the Delegator, was regarded as more noble than all other prelates, while he was exercising his power.[28] He was, therefore, in possession of all the rights of an ordinary officer with regard to further delegation

---

[27] C. 28, 43, X, *de officio et potestate iudicis delegati,* I, 29.

[28] C. II, X, *de officio et potestate iudicis delegati,* I, 29; Reiffenstuel, lib. I, tit. XXIX, n. 57 ss.

of his power. Hence, even if his power extended to one case alone, he could subdelegate.[29]

The legislation of the Code in the paragraph quoted above is identical with the pre-Code dispositions of law. In the Code, however, the *Delegatus a Principe* has been more specifically determined to be the Delegate of the Apostolic See. Consequently, a delegate who has received his power directly from the Roman Pontiff, and a delegate who has derived it from the Congregations, Tribunals or Offices through which the Pope is wont to administer the affairs of the universal Church, is in the new law truly a *Delegatus a Principe*.[30]

Previous to the Code, there was much doubt as to the competence of Ordinaries to subdelegate certain dispensatory faculties granted by the Holy See.[31] The Holy Office ended the difficulty by replying that the diocesan Bishop could subdelegate without any additional favor the delegated faculties of the Holy See, either habitually or for a particular case, unless the contrary was expressly stated in the rescript.[32] This response permits no similar doubt to arise with regard to the interpretation of the present canon of the Code.

The canon provides for two exceptions to the general rule; subdelegation is forbidden if it is so expressly stated in the original act of delegation, and also if the delegate has been chosen because of his special personal qualifications. In the first case, the Holy See in the act of delegation imposes a restriction which effectively prevents the delegate from sharing his power with others. The Code thus expressly forbids the subdelegation of the power of orders as a general rule, even though the original delegation has derived from the Holy See.[33] The second exception is that of a strictly personal delegation. The delegate is then said to have been chosen *industria personae;* that is, he is especially preferred to other possible selections because of certain personal qualifications which make him unusually suitable for the execution of the matter for which delegation is conceded. The *industria personae* does not signify

[29] Schmalzgrueber, lib. I, tit. XXIX, n. 10; D'Annibale, *Summula Theologiae Moralis,* I, n. 72, not. 20.

[30] Can. 7.

[31] Cf. Kinane, "Jurisdiction in the New Code," *IER,* XIII (1919), 206.

[32] S. C. S. Off., 14 Dec. 1898—*Coll.* n. 2029; Wernz, IV, n. 622, not. 104.

[33] Can. 210

merely the usual qualities of person or character that are demanded for a particular function. The very law of nature demands that power be not entrusted to a person who is not sufficiently competent to make proper use of it. But beyond this fitness and mere sufficiency, there may be special additional qualities that commend an individual. When a delegate is appointed with due consideration of these latter qualities, and because of them, he is said to be delegated *electa industria personae,* and he is incompetent to subdelegate. Thus, for example, a synodal judge skilled in medical matters, while his colleagues are not, might be said to be chosen because of his unusual knowledge, if he were delegated for all cases concerning the impediment of impotence that might occur in a diocese; similarly, a judge especially selected for all cases involving the impediment of disparity of cult, because of his expert theological knowledge on matters pertaining to the validity of the Sacraments.

Roberti [34] contends that delegation of judicial power must always be presumed to have been made *electa industria personae.* This opinion is untenable. It is true that judicial power cannot be delegated to a cleric who is not sufficiently skilled in matters of substantive law and procedure; but this is merely the natural demand that no incompetent person be endowed with power. The strictly personal delegation implies much more than this; it connotes qualities that are more than sufficient and a delegation precisely because of these qualities. The selection of a delegate in this manner must not be presumed; it is an additional fact that must be proved. Moreover, it is exactly with regard to delegated judges that the old authors discuss the application of the phrase *industria personae;* and they admit, in treating of the office and power of the delegated judge, that the delegate of the Supreme Pontiff may subdelegate his judicial power as a general rule, and regard as an exception the nomination of judges *electa industria personae.*[35] In this matter the Code has made no innovation; nor has Roberti advanced a single reason for his contention. It is, therefore, to be rejected.

[34] *De Processibus,* I, n. 147.

[35] Reiffenstuel, lib. I, tit. XXIX, n. 60; Schmalzgrueber, lib. I, tit. XXIX, n. 10; Wernz, II, n. 553; Bouix, *De Judiciis Ecclesiasticis,* I, 145; Santi, lib. I, tit. XXIX, n. 8.

In what manner, then, does it become clear that a delegate has been selected by reason of his special personal qualifications? Such a selection can be revealed by the express words of the delegator, indicating that the duty is to be performed personally by the delegate. Or it may be manifested tacitly by certain expressions which indicate the unusual gravity of the matter committed and the difficulty attendant upon its execution.[36] Authors generally regarded as a strictly personal delegation the committing to another of the *nudum ministerium*, since in this case the matter was already known to the delegator and resolved by him, only the execution of the same remaining to be effected.[37] This last instance is no longer admissible. Canon 57, §1, expressly concedes to the executor of rescripts, which frequently imply *nuda ministeria*, the right to substitute another in his place. Moreover, it is not at all clear that the Ordinary selects the executor of a *nudum ministerium* with the intention that he act personally. Consequently, Creusen [38] and Chelodi [39] do not enumerate the commission of the *nudum ministerium* among the examples of strictly personal delegation.

The dispositions of Canon 199 hitherto discussed have had to do with delegation and subdelegation in so far as the active subject is the Apostolic See. In the following two paragraphs, the canon deals with subdelegation of power derived from inferior prelates.

Can. 199, §3. **Potestas delegata ad universitatem negotiorum ab eo qui infra Romanum Pontificem habet ordinariam potestatem, potest in singulis casibus subdelegari.**

This text treats of the power to subdelegate enjoyed by one who has himself been delegated universally (*ad universitatem negotiorum*); such a delegate is hereby accorded the right to subdelegate in single cases. This principle was not contained

[36] V. g., "Negotium difficile et arduum committimus;" cf. DeRosa, *De Executoribus Litterarum Apostolicarum*, I, cap. IX, n. 43. Not, however, such phrases as, "conscientiam tuam onerantes, prudentiae tuae de qua specialiter confidimus;" cf. D'Annibale, *op. cit.*, I, n. 70, not. 20; Maroto, *Institutiones*, I, 846, not. 2.

[37] Schmalzgrueber, lib. I, tit. XXIX, n. 10; St. Alphonsus, VI, n. 566; Bouix, *De Judiciis Ecclesiasticis*, I, 145; Maroto, *op. cit.*, I, n. 707, B.

[38] Vermeersch-Creusen, *Epitome*, I, n. 280.

[39] *Jus de Personis*, n. 127.

in the Decretals and its origin must be sought in custom, based indeed on the interpretation of some passages in Roman Law.[40] The principle was rejected by Bouix[41] as unsafe; this author adhered to the principle that only the Delegate of the Supreme Ruler could subdelegate. Laymann,[42] St. Alphonsus,[43] and D'Annibale[44] taught a different doctrine on this matter. They contended that in general universal delegation could not be subdelegated; but if together with universal delegation an ecclesiastical office was granted to the delegate, subdelegation was possible, for in this case the power could be regarded as legally equivalent to ordinary power and hence delegable. Hence, they denied to assistant priests, delegated universally, the power to subdelegate it; if, however, during the absence of the pastor the pastoral office was entrusted to them, they could subdelegate.[45] These distinctions and doubts have been dispelled by the Code which has for the first time introduced the principle enunciated above into authorized ecclesiastical law.

Delegation is universal when it extends to at least a general class of acts which are within the power of the delegator. It is opposed to particular delegation which is given for one or more cases. Universal delegation implies a relation to quantity, or to the number of cases to which it extends; it is conceivable although restrictions have been made with regard to time, place or any other circumstance. Thus, a curate delegated to assist for one year at all marriages to be contracted between persons of a determined nationality who live in a determined section of a parish, may be regarded as a universal delegate, since his power extends to a class of indetermined acts, despite the restrictions of time, place and circumstances imposed on him.

The fourth paragraph of Canon 199 reads as follows:

In aliis casibus potestas iurisdictionis delegata subdelegari potest tantummodo ex concessione expresse facta, sed articulum aliquem non iurisdictionalem etiam sine expressa commissione iudices delegati possunt subdelegare.

---

[40] "De Potestate Delegata ad Universitatem Causarum deque ejus Subdelegabilitate," *Jus. Pont.*, VIII (1928), 183.

[41] *Op. cit.*, I, 146.

[42] *Theologia Moralis*, V, tr. 6, c. 10, n. 12.

[43] VI, n. 566.

[44] *Op. cit.*, I, n. 71.

[45] St. Alphonsus, *loc. cit.*

This text, by the words, *in aliis casibus,* makes it clear that here there is no question of the Delegate of the Holy See, nor of the delegate of any inferior to the Pope, who has been delegated universally. There is question, consequently, of the particular delegate of an inferior prelate. Such a delegate may not subdelegate; this is the rule. He may, however, subdelegate his power if the original delegator has conceded him the right; this is the exception. Since the ordinary magistrate may commit his power to whomsoever he would, it is his right to grant this faculty to subdelegate; the commission is then conceived as coming from the ordinary officer.[46]

The canon makes a further provision for delegated judges who have been named for particular cases by an inferior prelate. They may commit to others any non-jurisdictional act. The non-jurisdictional act corresponds to the *nudum ministerium.* The one to whom it is entrusted is an *executor;* he is not necessarily the *cognitor* nor need he have any legal knowledge of the merits of the case.[47] The swearing in of witnesses, investigations concerning facts of the case, collection of a fine, and similar acts, are non-jurisdictional.[48]

It is noteworthy that in allowing the commission of non-jurisdictional articles to others, the Code has mentioned explicitly delegated judges. It is not clear why the legislator has permitted such a thing to judges, and not to other delegates. The executor of a non-jurisdictional act exercises no jurisdiction and it does not seem as though a special concession of law is required in order that delegates, who are not judges, might commit such acts to another. Since there is no explicit prohibition that would prevent delegates, who are not judges, from committing to others non-jurisdictional acts, and since explicit provision for such commitment is lacking in the Code, some authors [49] have concluded that also those delegated for voluntary matters may entrust to others non-jurisdictional acts.

The present canon gives rise to a difficulty, when it is compared with Canon 57, §1, which provides that the executor of a

[46] Wernz-Vidal, *Jus Canonicum,* II, n. 371.

[47] C. 27, X, *de officio et potestate iudicis delegati,* I, 29; Reiffenstuel, lib. I, tit. XXIX, n. 64.

[48] Noval, *De Judiciis,* n. 182; Vermeersch-Creusen, *op. cit.,* I, n. 280, 4.

[49] Chelodi, *Jus de Personis,* p. 205; *Jus Pont.,* VIII (1928), 190; cf. can. 20.

rescript may substitute another in the execution of the same. Now, sometimes it happens that a rescript is granted for a particular case by a prelate inferior to the Holy See, v.g., by a Bishop; moreover, the rescript may so be granted that the executor is free to execute, or not to execute, as he deems expedient. In such a case, the executor has not merely a *nudum ministerium* to perform; more than this, he is truly a delegate, enjoying a power of jurisdiction to be used or not to be used at his discretion.[50] Hence, if such an executor is truly a delegate and enjoys the right to make use of a substitute in the execution of the rescript, as Canon 57, §1, would seem to permit, the nomination of the substitute would be an act of subdelegation. On the other hand, Canon 199, §4, would prohibit subdelegation, because in the hypothesis it is question of a particular delegation granted, not by the Holy See, but by a Bishop. There is, therefore, an apparent contradiction. Either the executor of an episcopal rescript granting particular delegation can subdelegate, or he cannot; if he can, Canon 57, §1, prevails over Canon 199, §4; if he cannot, the contrary is true.

It must be remembered that a rescript can be granted *in forma gratiosa*; it is then conceded immediately to the petitioner and no executor is required. Or it may be granted *in forma commissoria*; it is then committed to an executor. The latter is sometimes a *necessary*, sometimes a *voluntary* executor. The necessary executor is so called because he is obliged to execute the rescript, unless evident defects, well determined by the legislator, postulate the contrary.[51] He has received a favor already granted (*gratia facta*) and his task is a *nudum ministerium.* On the contrary, a voluntary executor is free to execute or not to execute, according to the merits of the case. It is question of a favor not yet granted (*gratia facienda*). The Bishop has merely remitted to him the petition for favor and has granted the power necessary to execute the request.[52] He is, therefore, truly a delegate.

How, then, reconcile the two canons in question? Clearly, there is no conflict between them when Canon 57, §1, is under-

[50] Maroto, *Institutiones,* I, n. 288, B; Chelodi, *op. cit.*, p. 132, not. 5; Blat, *Commentarium,* I, n. 119.

[51] Can. 54, §1.

[52] D'Annibale, *op. cit.,* I, n. 222; Chelodi, *op. cit.*, p. 132; Badii, *Institutiones,* n. 70.

stood to refer to the *necessary* executor of a particular, episcopal rescript, for he is not a delegate. At least that much is certain. But what of the *voluntary* executor who is truly a delegate, according to the notions exposed above? In this case there is a contradiction. The solution of the question depends on a further question: Is the canon on rescripts more general than that on delegation, or is the contrary true? *Generi per speciem derogatur.*[53]

Kinane[54] states that Canon 57 "must be regarded as correcting the more general principle of Canon 199, §4." But is the latter canon more general? It does not seem so. In addition to the fact that Canon 57, §1, is found under the inscription of the Code, *Normae Generales,* it is true that this canon refers to both Apostolic and episcopal rescripts, and to both general and particular rescripts. On the other hand, Canon 199, §4, does not refer to Apostolic delegation but only to inferior and particular delegation.[55] Hence, Canon 57, §1, seems to be more general than the later canon. The contrary could be true only for one reason, namely, because delegation may be written or oral, while rescripts are always written. This contention cannot be urged; for Canon 206, treating of successive delegates, states the matter should be executed by him whose mandate was first granted, unless it has been expressly abrogated by a later *rescript.* No one will contend that delegation, granted orally, must be revoked by written document, in order that the revocation be valid. The canon evidently presupposes a *written* concession of delegation. From this it does not follow that all delegation must be given in writing; the Code expressly states that confessional jurisdiction may be granted orally.[56] But this much is clear; the legislator, treating professedly of delegation in Canon 206, speaks of it as a concession made in writing. If he has presupposed this in Canon 206, is it possible that he supposes different in Canon 199, when no possible reason for a distinction can be conceived? Hence, delegation should *regularly* be given in writing, and this is the mind of the legislator implied in all the canons treating *ex professo* of delegation.

---

[53] Reg. 34, R. J., in VI.
[54] *IER,* XIII (1919), 209.
[55] Cf. can. 199, §4, "In aliis casibus . . . ;" vide, §§2-3.
[56] Can. 879, §1.

Moreover, there is no juridical reason to sustain the view that, if delegation is given in writing, the delegate may subdelegate, according to Canon 57, §1; if it is given orally for a particular case, he may not subdelegate, according to Canon 199, §4. Such a distinction would be juridically inane. Hence, it is to be concluded that Canon 57 is more general and is restricted by the canon on delegation. Therefore, even if the delegation has been granted by rescript, if it is for a particular case and derives from an inferior of the Pope, the executor cannot subdelegate his duty. There is no room for doubt when one considers that Canon 57, §1, makes provision for a contrary disposition of law (*nisi substitutio prohibita fuerit*); but substitution is forbidden in the case of a particular delegation, emanating from a prelate inferior to the Roman Pontiff by Canon 199, §4.

It is true that many authors, commenting on Canon 57, §1, do not induce any restriction; but since they do not take cognizance of the difficulty, their assertions have little value with regard to this point.[57] At least two authors, Blat[58] and Mostaza,[59] have seen fit to restrict Canon 57, §1, in order to prevent the destruction of Canon 199, §4. The latter authors understand the first canon to apply solely to Apostolic rescripts, so that only the executor of an Apostolic rescript could substitute another person in carrying out his duty. This interpretation without necessity excludes the executor of a rescript that is not Apostolic in which a *gratia facta* is contained; whereas Canon 199, §4, only compels the exclusion of the executer of a *gratia facienda*, since he alone is truly a delegate. In reconciling conflicting canons that interpretation must be selected which least derogates from the principle stated therein. It is sufficient to maintain that merely a particular delegate of a prelate inferior to the Holy See is excluded from Canon 57, §1.

The Church has, therefore, at her discrete disposal, the licit

***Can. 199, §5.* Nulla subdelegata potestas potest iterum subdelegari, nisi id expresse concessum fuerit.**

This text defines the ultimate extent to which subdelegation

[57] Cf. Cicognani, *Commentarium ad Librum I Codicis*, p. 260; Cocchi, *Commentarium,* I, n. 112; Maroto, *op. cit.*, I, 334.

[58] *Commentarium,* I, n. 122.

[59] *Annotationes Privatae,* Romae, 1928, p. 166.

may be conceded. No subdelegated power, even if it originally came from the Holy See, can again be subdelegated, unless express permission to do so has been granted by the ordinary officer.[60]

Article II—The Passive Subject of Delegation

The Code has not directly legislated on the qualities required in the delegate. The older authors were wont to sum them up in the following verse:

> Liber, mas, gnarus, cui sit mens, integra fama,
> Aetas, qui subsit: committitur huic bene causa.

Like the delegator, the passive subject must be capable of a human act. Females and infidels are incapable of exercising ecclesiastical jurisdiction, while an inferior of the Roman Pontiff would invalidly delegate the same to the laity.[61] In order that delegation be licit, the passive subject must be competent to exercise the power that is committed to him; this does not signify he must be more skilled than others, but that he must be sufficiently equipped mentally and morally. The old law[62] forbade the delegation of judicial power to delegates under twenty years of age; if the parties consented, the age of eighteen years sufficed; delegates under eighteen could be delegated only by the Pope. The present legislation makes no mention of age. The delegate, moreover, must not be under ecclesiastical censure, since the acts of such a delegate would be illicit or invalid, according to the provisions of the law in specific cases.[63] Finally, the Code requires determined qualities in the passive subject in specific matters. Thus, synodal judges must be priests of good morals, who are skilled in canon law,[64] while the confessors of religious women must regularly be forty years of age.[65]

A question of importance in connection with the delegate is whether or not acceptance of delegation is required for the validity of the same. It is quite certain that delegation granted

---

[60] Vermeersch-Creusen, *Epitome,* I, n. 280, 5.

[61] Maroto, *Institutiones,* I, n. 708.

[62] C. 41, X, *de officio et potestate iudicis delegati,* I, 29.

[63] Cf. can. 2264; 2284; Hyland, *Excommunication,* p. 146 ss.

[64] Can. 1574, §1.

[65] Can. 524, §1.

by law or general statute requires no acceptance in order that it be valid.[66] If delegation is granted in the presence of the delegate, silence implies tacit consent.[67] Again, if delegation is asked for by a priest through the medium of another person, the act dependent upon that delegation will be valid, if it is executed after the delegation has actually been granted but before the concession has been intimated to the delegate; the act will, however, be illicit.[68] The same may be said of the case in which the delegate has not himself requested the faculty, but knows that another has sought it for him.[69] In all these cases acceptance is tacit or implied.

A more serious difficulty arises in the case in which the delegation is granted by the delegator spontaneously (*motu proprio*), without any requests having preceded, or in the case in which the power is sought by a third party without the knowledge of the cleric actually delegated. In such cases implicit acceptance is out of the question. Is such delegation valid? The following case will make more manifest the nature of the difficulty: Father Adrian is to assist at a marriage in a mission church; through a misunderstanding he falsely believes he has been delegated by the pastor of the place. In the meantime, a third party, realizing the difficulty, seeks delegation from the Bishop for Father Adrian, who is still unaware of the defect. When knowledge of the episcopal delegation is brought to Father Adrian, the marriage ceremony has already taken place. It is certain, however, that the Bishop granted the faculty some hours before the ceremony. In this case, the marriage can be valid only if the acceptance of the episcopal delegation was not required for the validity of the same.

Before the Code a very common opinion held that acceptance of delegation was necessary for validity.[70] The reason for this opinion was because delegation was regarded as a sort of *dona-*

---

[66] Wernz-Vidal, *Jus Canonicum*, V, 634, not. 46.

[67] "Qui tacet, consentire videtur,"—Reg. 43, R. J., in VI; Gasparri, *De Matrimonio*, II, n. 944.

[68] Gasparri, *loc. cit.* Cf. can. 53.

[69] Cappello, *De Sacramentis*, III, n. 675; Wernz-Vidal, *op. cit.*, V, n. 538.

[70] Gasparri, *op. cit.*, II, n. 944; Wernz, IV, n. 180; D'Annibale, *op. cit.*, I, n. 72; Lehmkuhl, *Theologia Moralis*, II, n. 777; Sanchez, *De Sancto Matrimonii Sacramento*, I, disp. 36, n. 1 ss.

tion, which has its effect only after acceptance.[71] Vlaming[72] regards knowledge and acceptance of delegation as a postulate of the very notion of delegation, since without them the bond between delegator and delegate, in virtue of which the latter would act as delegate, would be completely lacking.

This common opinion was based on two decisions of the Sacred Congregation of the Council. On December 5, 1926, the Congregation decided: *posita ignorantia licentiae, matrimonium non esse validum;* again, on April 15, 1628, a similar decision was rendered.[73] Despite the decisions of the Congregation and the common opinion of authors, the controversy was not ended. Indeed, so keen was it, that in 1911 the Rota, reviewing a similar case, and recalling the decisions of the Sacred Congregation, refused to render a sentence of invalidity, precisely because of the legal doubts existing on the matter.[74] Such a decision, rendered only a short time before the promulgation of the Code, manifests the gravity of the opinion of Engel, Scherer, and others who denied the necessity of the knowledge or acceptance of delegation.

The Code has not dispelled the doubts. Since its promulgation the majority of authors have adhered to the opinion so prevalent before. A few authors,[75] however, have deduced further argument to sustain the less common opinion. By force of Canon 37 a rescript is valid before its acceptance, even if it is sought without the assent of him to whom it is granted (*praeter eius assensum*). Hence, a rescript, including one of delegation,[76] is valid if it is sought without the knowledge of the person actually delegated. It is significant that the pro- visions of Canon 37 are regarded as an innovation by Cocchi[77] while Ojetti[78] states that it is a departure from the usu principle. Hence, if in the matter of rescripts the need of a ceptance has been done away with by the Code, it is logical

[71] Wernz, IV, n. 180, not. 218.

[72] *Praelectiones Juris Matrimonii,* II, n. 573.

[73] Pallotini, XIII, V. *Matrimonium,* XVI, n. 52 ss.

[74] 20 Jan. 1911, *Casu Divionensi,—AAS,* III (1911), 284 ss.

[75] Aertnys-Damen, *Theologia Moralis,* II, n. 837; Cappello, *op. cit.,* II, n. 391.

[76] Gappello, *loc. cit.*

[77] *Commentarium,* I, n. 104.

[78] *Commentarium,* I, 212.

contend that acceptance of delegation, whether granted by rescript or by word of mouth, is no longer required for the validity of the same.

The problem remains shrouded in doubt, as it was before the Code. The Code has given more weight to the less common opinion, but not sufficient to afford any degree of certitude. Hence, a *dubium iuris* exists in this matter, and by virtue of Canon 15 it is to be concluded that acceptance is not required for validity. Therefore, the marriage performed by Father Adrian, as proposed above, must be regarded as valid.

Article III—The Subject of the Power of Orders

The power of orders is partly of divine right, partly of human right. The Church is incompetent to legislate concerning the valid exercise of that power of orders which is of divine right. Thus, no ecclesiastical law can make invalid the Holy Sacrifice that is validly celebrated by a validly ordained priest, nor can any human law render invalid an ordination that has been validly conferred by a validly consecrated Bishop. With regard to such powers the Church is competent to decree only what pertains to their licit exercise, as is the case when she legislates concerning vestments to be worn, rubrics to be observed, and the like.

There are, however, powers of orders of merely human right, and in these the Church is eminently and exclusively competent; since she has originated them, she can change, suspend, or abolish them. According to the common teaching, all orders, other than the episcopacy, priesthood and diaconate, are of ecclesiastical origin.[79]

There can be no question of the delegation of that power of orders which is of divine right. Since such a power is acquired by ordination which imprints a character on the soul, it is strictly personal and cannot be shared with others. Hence, not even the Supreme Pontiff could commit to a minor cleric the power to ordain a priest, since the power acquired by divine law would be lacking. There may, however, be question of committing to others the right to exercise licitly this divine power.

---

[79] Gasparri, *De Sacra Ordinatione*, I, n. 33; Cappello, *Summa Juris Publici*, p. 185, not. 6.

Thus, although any Bishop may validly ordain priests, only some Bishops may do so licitly, since the right to ordain is reserved to the proper Bishop of the cleric to be ordained. The proper Bishop, however, may in certain circumstances entrust this right to another Bishop, so that the latter licitly, as well as validly, might ordain.

In the matter of the power of orders of ecclesiastical right, an entirely different disposition prevails. The Church may delegate not only the exercise of this power, but also the power itself, since this is entirely of ecclesiastical disposition. Thus, the very power that is attached to minor orders could be committed to the laity at the discretion of the Supreme Pontiff. Since, however, the Church has instituted orders *ad instar sacramentorum,* she is not wont to commit such powers to persons who have not acquired the corresponding right through the usual channel of ordination.[80]

The Church has, therefore, at her discrete disposal, the licit exercise of the orders of divine right, and both the power, and the exercise of the power, of orders of human origin. In disposing of these, she may entrust them directly to persons; the powers or rights so entrusted may be called *delegated.* Or she may entrust them by law to ecclesiastical offices, in which case they may be called *ordinary.*

The concepts here proposed will be of assistance for the interpretation of the following canon:

Can. 210. **Potestas ordinis, a legitimo Superiore ecclesiastico sive adnexa officio sive commissa personae, nequit aliis demandari, nisi id expresse fuerit iure vel indulto concessum.**

The legislator speaks of the power of orders which the legitimate ecclesiastical Superior has either attached to an office or entrusted to a person. Therefore, in the matter of orders of divine right, there can be question only of so annexing to an office or committing to a person the right to exercise licitly powers which the Church cannot prevent from being exercised validly. Thus, the Code reserves to the office of Supreme

[80] "De Delegationibus et Subdelegationibus Ecclesiasticis," *Jus Pont.,* III (1923), 86-91; n. 11.

Pontiff the right to consecrate Bishops;[81] hence, the Pope alone may be said to enjoy this right as an ordinary power, although all Bishops are competent to render valid episcopal consecration. On the other hand, the power of orders of human right can be entrusted to whomsoever the Pope wishes; hence, the canon may be understood of the commission of the very power itself as well as the exercise of that power.

In either case, the power of orders or the right to exercise that power cannot be committed to others by those who enjoy the power or right in virtue of a disposition of law attaching the same to their office, or in virtue of commission made personally to them by the competent Superior. In other words, the general principles of delegation are not applicable to the power of orders; so that, even if a commission has proceeded from the Holy See, the person so commissioned is incapable of entrusting his acquired power to another, while the same prohibition affects equally well those who enjoy such powers as ordinary.

The canon provides for contrary dispositions to be made either in law or by indult. Thus, the law permits Bishops who are impeded from ordaining their own subjects, to entrust the ordination of the same to other Bishops.[82] Similar provisions can be made by particular indults.

The active subject, then, of delegation of the power of orders is always the Holy See, except in cases provided for by law or by indult when inferiors may commit to others such power. The passive subject of that power of orders which is of divine right, must always be an ecclesiastical person endowed with the sacred order corresponding to the power he is about to exercise. The passive subject of the power of orders of human right may be any subject of the Church; regularly, however, it is only an ecclesiastical person who has acquired the corresponding power by ordination.

By virtue of this canon simple priests, who lack the episcopal character, may not delegate to others the faculty of administering the Sacrament of Confirmation or of conferring minor orders, if they enjoy such by disposition of law or by indult.[83]

---

[81] Can. 953.

[82] Can. 955, §2.

[83] Cf. can. 294, §2; 957, §2; 782, §2.

CHAPTER VII

THE EXERCISE OF DELEGATION

The legislator has established in several successive canons principles that regulate the exercise or use of jurisdiction. Some such principles apply to all jurisdiction, some only to ordinary jurisdiction, some to delegated jurisdiction exclusively. Whatever refers merely to ordinary jurisdiction, lies beyond the pale of this work. In the following pages a brief commentary on those canons which refer either explicitly or implicitly to the exercise of delegated power will be attempted.

ARTICLE I—THE INTERPRETATION OF DELEGATION

The Code first provides a principle for the practical solution of doubts that might arise regarding the extent of delegated power. It is, as it were, a reflex principle, by virtue of which the delegate might proceed with security in the exercise of his power. Before the Code all delegation was regarded as odious, since by it the delegate acted with authority which was exclusively that of the ordinary officer and thus derogated to a certain degree the exclusive rights of the same.[1] The legislator has, therefore, introduced an innovation, as follows:

Can. 200, §1. **Potestas iurisdictionis ordinaria et ad universitatem negotiorum delegata, late interpretanda est; alia quaelibet stricte; cui tamen delegata potestas est, ea quoque intelliguntur concessa, sine quibus eadem exerceri non posset.**

§2. **Ei, qui delegatum se asserit, incumbit onus probandae delegationis.**

In virtue of this canon delegation which is universal (*ad universitatem negotiorum*), is not odious, but favorable, and

[1] Kinane, "Jurisdiction in the New Code", *IER,* XIII (1919), 209.

consequently subject to a broad interpretation. The reason for this disposition is because universal delegation is legally assimilated to ordinary power; ordinary power, however, admits of broad interpretation since it is derogative of the rights of no one, and favors regularly are to be extended. Hence, in doubt the more favorable interpretation is to be accepted, as long as the interpretation is not extended beyond the proper juridical meaning of the terms employed in the mandate.[2] All other delegation must be strictly interpreted, for by such the delegator cedes a certain restricted quantity of power to be exercised in one or more particular cases, and he is not presumed to have granted more than the strict tenor of the mandate implies. Since the canon has not distinguished, it must be said that particular delegation that derives from the Apostolic See, must likewise be strictly interpreted.

The first paragraph of this canon further states that delegation implicitly includes the concession of all means necessary for the exercise of the same. This principle is not new, since the *Regulae Iuris* of Boniface VIII contained similar provisions.[3] It is in virtue of this principle that a delegated judge is competent to adopt coactive means, when they are necessary for the execution of his mandate.[4]

The second paragraph of this canon asserts that the burden of proving his delegation rests upon anyone who asserts that he has been so delegated. This is an application of the principle that facts are not presumed but must be established. This proof of delegation is made possible when delegation is granted, as regularly it should be, in writing. However, any other legal method of proving facts can also establish the fact of delegation.

Article II—The Use of Delegation

The canons which treat of the actual use of delegation, first determine the persons over whom delegated power may be exercised; secondly, the forum in which the exercise of delegated power produces its effect; thirdly, the limits beyond which the

---

[2] Vermeersch-Creusen, *Epitome,* I, n. 93.

[3] "Plus semper in se continet, quod est minus,"—Reg. 35; "Cui licet, quod est plus, licet utique, quod est minus,"—Reg. 53; "in toto partem, non est dubium contineri,"—Reg. 80.

[4] Maroto, *Institutiones,* I, n. 711, 1; cf. can. 66, §3.

delegate must not act in exercising his power; and finally, the powers of the delegate during the period in which recourse is being made to the Superior. These details will be treated in the following paragraphs.

§1. The Persons Over Whom Delegation May Be Exercised

In Canon 201 the legislator first states a general principle:

Can. 201, §1. **Potestas iurisdictionis potest in solos subditos directe exerceri.**

The power of jurisdiction, whether it is ordinary or delegated, judicial or voluntary, can be exercised directly over subjects alone. A delegate, since he acts in the name and place of the delegator, acquires to himself the subjects of the delegator, in so far as his mandate extends to them, and no further. The principle involved in this paragraph is the fact that jurisdiction implies a relation of Superior and subject; it is not exercised over inanimate objects, contracts, judicial causes, or the like, but it is exercised over persons who have some relation to the Superior, either immediately, or mediately, through some juridical fact. Hence, the relation of Superior and subject is not necessarily a permanent one, but it may arise from a juridical fact of a transient nature and thus be dissolved with the cessation of the same fact.[5]

The Code here merely asserts a general principle and makes no effort to determine specifically who are subjects. The common manner of establishing the relation of Superior and subject is by the acquisition of domicile or quasi-domicile.[6] Those who have not even a quasi-domicile in any place, are subjects of the Ordinary in whose terrritory they actually remain;[7] such are called *vagi.* Those who possess at least a quasi-domicile, are called *peregrini* as long as they are outside the territory of their domicile, or quasi-domicile.[8] Such persons frequently become subjects of the Ordinary in whose territory they temporarily remain, with regard to certain specified matters. Thus, ap-

[5] Wernz-Vidal, *Jus Canonicum,* II, n. 375.
[6] Can. 94, §1.
[7] Can. 91; 94, §2.
[8] Can. 91.

proved confessors of a determined place can absolve such travellers.[9] Ordinaries can dispense them from certain matrimonial impediments when they are found in danger of death,[10] while pastors and other priests may do the same in certain circumstances.[11] Ordinaries and pastors may dispense them from the law on the observance of feasts, fast and abstinence,[12] while the same power is extended to the Superiors of a clerical exempt religion.[13] All these acts imply the exercise of jurisdiction over temporary sojourners who must consequently be said to be subjects of the person exercising jurisdiction, since jurisdiction can be exercised exclusively over subjects.

In the matter of ordination of seculars, he alone is subject to a Bishop's jurisdiction, who has within the diocese his place of origin together with domicile;[14] here, there is no question of quasi-domicile. Domicile without origin will suffice only when the candidate confirms by oath his intention of remaining perpetually in the diocese. In the matter of assistance at marriage, a sojourn of one month is sufficient to establish the necessary relation to the Superior, and in the case of those who nowhere have even a quasi-domicile, actual existence in the place is enough.[15]

It is well to recall that a cleric may become incardinated into a diocese in which he has never actually been present and thus by incardination become a direct subject of another Bishop.[16] Hence, residence even of a brief duration is not always required to establish the relation of Superior and subject.

In the exercise of judicial jurisdiction a superior becomes competent in many unusual manners. The general rule regarding domicile and quasi-domicile prevails,[17] and *vagi* may be tried in the place of actual sojourn.[18] But a departure from the usual norms is found in the matter of contracts. Thus, the place where a contract has been entered upon, or even the place

[9] Can. 881, §1.
[10] Can. 1043.
[11] Can. 1044; 1045.
[12] Can. 1245, §1.
[13] Can. 1245, §3; 514, §1.
[14] Can. 90, §1; 956.
[15] Can. 1097, §§1-2.
[16] Can. 111, §2.
[17] Can. 1561.
[18] Can. 1563.

wherein the same is to be fulfilled, becomes the forum for disputes between the contracting parties with regard to that contract,[19] as long as the defendant has not withdrawn from that territory.[20] Moreover, the contracting parties are even free to choose at the time the contract is made a forum wherein the defendant can be cited and convened, even should he be absent from that territory.[21] Such instances could be multiplied indefinitely; a glance at the title on the Competent Forum in the Fourth Book of the Code will reveal various manners in which persons come under the judicial jurisdiction of ecclesiastical Superiors.[22]

Creusen [23] regards the exercise of jurisdiction in the instances mentioned in the above paragraph as indirect. This does not seem correct. The Superior merely acquires subjects in a temporary manner by reason of contract, delict, benefice, and the like. The jurisdiction is directly exercised over the subjects thus acquired. This is the teaching of D'Annibale,[24] who states that if travellers have violated laws protective of public peace in the place where they are actually present, they for that very reason become *subjects by reason of their crime* (*subditos ratione delicti*). Similarly, therefore, the same effect is produced by other juridical facts mentioned above. Jurisdiction is said to be exercised indirectly, when by directly exercising it over subjects the Superior indirectly affects non-subjects.

The present canon does not exclude the indirect exercise of jurisdiction over non-subjects. Thus, the Holy See dispensing a subject from the impediment of disparity of cult indirectly affects the infidel, who cannot be a subject; similarly, a Bishop who dispenses a subject from the impediment of consanguinity in order that marriage might be contracted with a subject of another diocese, indirectly exercises jurisdiction over one who is not his subject.

The Code, having stated a general principle with regard to the exercise of jurisdiction, next aptly distinguishes between

19 Can. 1565, §1.

20 Pont. Comm. ad CC. auth. Interpret.,—14 Jul. 1922—*AAS* XIV (1922), 529.

21 Can. 1565, §2.

22 Can. 1560-1568.

23 Vermeersch-Creusen, *Epitome,* I, n. 282.

24 *Summula Theologiae Moralis,* I, n. 86.

judicial and voluntary jurisdiction. Concerning the former this principle is enunciated:

Can. 201, §2. **Iudicialis potestas tam ordinaria quam delegata exerceri nequit in proprium commodum aut extra teritorium, salvis praescriptis can. 201, §1, 881, §2, et 1637.**

This paragraph deals exclusively with *judicial* power which is that power which is exercised in a judicial process. In the following paragraph the legislator describes *voluntary* jurisdiction as *non-judicial (potestatem iurisdictionis voluntariam seu non-iudicialem).* Hence, the term *voluntary jurisdiction* must be regarded in a very wide sense as all jurisdiction that is not properly judicial. It includes, therefore, not only the power to dispense or grant favors, but also the power to legislate and apply coaction.[25]

The paragraph quoted states two things: first, the possessor of judicial power cannot exercise the same for his own utility. This is an evident consequence of the nature of judicial power, since no one can be a good judge in his own case; secondly, the possessor of judicial power cannot make use of it when he is outside his legitimate territory, according to the old principle, *Extra territorium ius dicenti impune non paretur.*[26] The territory, in the exercise of the delegated power, signifies the territory of the delegator, unless the latter has assigned to the delegate only a restricted portion of that territory; in the latter case, the delegate cannot exercise his power outside the determined territory.

The same paragraph admits of certain exceptions to the rule established. Since penitential jurisdiction is truly judicial, actual exceptions to the rule have been established when the legislator determined that the Canon Penitentiary may absolve his diocesans outside the confines of his proper diocese,[27] and that the possessor of ordinary power to absolve from sins may make use of his power in absolving his subjects in any part of the world.[28] A third exception is made for the case of the

[25] Hilling, "Die Bedeutung der iurisdictio voluntaria und involuntaria in römischen Recht und im kanonischen Recht des Mittelalters und der Neuzeit," *AkKR,* CV (1925), 469 ss.

[26] C. 2, *de constitutionibus,* I, 2, in VI.

[27] Can. 401, §2.

[28] Can. 881, §2.

judge who is forcefully expelled from his territory or prevented from exercising his jurisdiction therein; he is permitted to exercise it outside the territory, after having informed the Ordinary of the place concerning what he is about to do.[29] This third exception bears directly on the question of delegation, unlike the first two which treat only of ordinary power. In speaking of the judge in this case the legislator has not distinguished; hence, the delegated judge enjoys the same privilege as the ordinary judge.[30]

When it is question of the exercise of voluntary power, the dispositions of law are entirely different.

Can. 201, §3. **Nisi aliud ex rerum natura aut ex iure constet, potestatem iurisdictionis voluntariam seu non-iudicialem quis exercere potest etiam in proprium commodum, aut extra territorium existens, aut in subditum e territorio absentem.**

This principle refers to the delegate as well as to the ordinary officer. Either may exercise voluntary jurisdiction in his own behalf, dispensing himself from a law in which he is competent to dispense, or granting himself the use of a privilege which it is within his power to give. Moreover, he may exercise such power when he himself is outside his territory, or he may use it in behalf of a subject who is actually outside the territory, as long as the relation of Superior and subject persists. This provision is made explicit in specific cases in the Code, as in the matter of dispensing from the law on observance of feasts, fast and abstinence, and from matrimonial impediments in danger of death.[31] Finally, a Superior, absent from his territory, may exercise voluntary jurisdiction over his subjects who are likewise absent from their proper territory. The canon does not say this expressly, but there is no reason why the several partitions of the third paragraph may not be taken conjunctively in this sense.[32]

It is to be noted that in the old law a Superior could not exercise jurisdiction over one of his subjects who was absent

[29] Can. 163.

[30] Noval, *De Judiciis,* n. 233; Roberti, *De Processibus,* I, n. 184.

[31] Can. 1245, §1; 1043.

[32] Blat, *Commentarium,* II, n. 150.

from his proper territory; nor could a Superior regularly exercise the same over a traveller who actually was present in the territory of the same Superior. This, of course, did not exclude exercise of power over *vagos*.[33] The present canon has, therefore, induced some opportune innovations.

The stipulations of this paragraph constitute a general rule which admits of exceptions that may arise from the nature of the matters in question or from positive law (*nisi aliud ex rerum natura aut ex iure constet . . .*). Thus, one competent to absolve from certain censures could not absolve himself from the same; nor may anyone confer on himself a benefice.[34]

§2. *The Forum for the Exercise of Jurisdiction*

The term *forum* is defined in the Decretals as *exercendarum litium locus a fando dictus, sive a Foreneo rege, qui primus leges Graecis dedit.*[35] It designates properly the *place* for the exercise of judicial power. By extension the term has come to mean, not only *local place,* but also the *sphere* in which power is exercised. The Code recognizes two such spheres, the external and the internal. Jurisdiction of the *external* forum directly refers to the public and common good of the Church, and is exercised publicly with social and juridical effects.[36] Jurisdiction of the internal forum refers primarily and directly to the private good of the faithful, regulates man's moral relations with God, and is exercised occultly with effects produced before God alone. This forum is called the *forum of conscience* by the legislator.[37] Jurisdiction of the internal forum may be *sacramental,* or *extra-sacramental;* the first is exercised only in the tribunal of Penance in the act of sacramental confession; the second is used outside that tribunal, but occultly with no effects produced in the external forum. Before the Code, a different terminology was used. The external forum was the *forum fori;* the internal was the *forum poli.*[38] The latter was either *penitential* or *extra-penitential.*[39]

---

[33] D'Annibale, *op. cit.,* I, n. 74.

[34] Can. 1437.

[35] C. 10, X, *de verborum significatione,* V, 40.

[36] Benedict XIV, *De Synodo Dioecesana,* XII, c. 1, n. 7.

[37] Can. 196.

[38] C. 43, C. XVII, q. 4.

[39] Wernz, II, 14.

The Code has legislated as follows concerning the *fora:*

Can. 202, §1. **Actus potestatis iurisdictionis sive ordinariae sive delegatae collatae pro foro externo, valet quoque pro interno, non autem e converso.**

§2. **Potestas collata pro foro interno exerceri potest etiam in foro interno extra-sacramentali, nisi sacramentale exigatur.**

§3. **Si forum, pro quo potestas data est, expressum non fuerit, potestas intelligitur concessa pro utroque foro, nisi ex ipsa rei natura aliud constet.**

These principles can briefly be stated, in so far as they pertain to delegation, as follows:

a. Delegation granted for the external forum may be exercised also in the internal forum, while that granted for the internal forum cannot be exercised in the external forum.

b. Delegation granted for the internal forum may be exercised sacramentally or extra-sacramentally, unless the sacramental forum is expressly prescribed.

c. Delegation granted without mention of forum is presumed to be conceded for both external and internal forum, unless the nature of the matter postulates otherwise. Thus, a faculty granted by the Sacred Penitentiary to absolve from censure, from the very nature of that tribunal, would validly be exercised in the internal forum exclusively.[40] Similarly, a faculty to dispense, granted to confessors, can be exercised only in the internal forum, since it is only here that a priest is actually a confessor.[41]

§3. *The Limits of Delegation*

From the nature of delegation it follows that the delegate enjoys no more authority than has been given to him. The following canon is a logical deduction:

Can. 203, §1. **Delegatus qui sive circa res sive circa personas mandati sui fines excedit, nihil agit.**

§2. **Hos tamen excessisse non intelligitur delegatus, qui alio modo ac deleganti placuerit, ea ad quae delegatus est,**

[40] Can. 258, §1.

[41] V. g., can. 1044.

peragit, nisi modus ipse fuerit a delegante praescriptum tanquam conditio.

The delegate acts invalidly, whenever he exceeds the limits imposed on him, either with regard to persons or things, by the delegator. Thus, if a priest delegated to hear the confessions of children should attempt to absolve adults, the latter would invalidly be absolved.

The principle must be accepted in the sense that the delegate acts invalidly in so far as he *exceeds* his mandate. Hence, if he has delegated power to dispense from the law of fast and abstinence, and he actually dispenses on the occasion of a nuptial festivity both from this law and from the impediment of mixed religion, over which he has no authority, the first dispensation is not invalid because the delegate has exceeded his mandate in granting the second, according to the principle: *Utile non debet per inutile vitiari.*[42]

It is to be noted that the delegate does not exceed his mandate, if in executing the same he makes use of the means necessary for that execution, since this right is conceded to him by the Code.[43]

The second paragraph of the canon treats of the manner of exercising delegation. Ordinarily, the delegate is obliged to execute his mandate in the manner prescribed by the delegator. If he does not, he acts illicitly, but validly, since the delegator is not presumed to decree a particular method of execution under the penalty of invalidity. The delegator may, however, so ordain. In this case the manner of executing the mandate is a *condition* required for the validity of the act. In law essential conditions are expressed by the particles *si, dummodo,* and the like.[44]

§4. *The Use of Delegation During Recourse*

Recourse here does not necessarily signify extra-judicial appeal to a Superior made after the inferior has acted, but it means any extra-judicial approach to the Superior by which a competent inferior is ignored, whether the latter has begun to

---

[42] Reg. 37, R. J., in VI.
[43] Can. 200, §1.
[44] Can. 39.

act or not. When one so approaches the Superior, the following is to be said concerning the power of the inferior:

Can. 204, §1. **Quod quis Superiorem adit, inferiore praetermisso, non idcirco voluntaria suspenditur inferioris potestas, sive haec ordinaria fuerit sive delegata.**

§2. **Attamen rei ad Superiorem delatae ne se immisceat inferior, nisi ex gravi urgentique causa; et hoc in casu statim Superiorem de re moneat.**

Voluntary jurisdiction is not suspended in the case when a person has passed over an inferior, whether the latter be Ordinary or delegate, and approached the Superior. The second paragraph provides that in such a case the inferior should refrain from acting, unless a grave and urgent reason for so acting is actually present; in the latter situation the inferior must inform the Superior that he is proceeding in the matter despite the recourse. It is obvious that the tenets of the second paragraph are prescribed only for the licitness of the procedure. In Canon 1048 Ordinaries are admonished not to use their faculties to dispense from matrimonial impediments, if a petition for such a dispensation has been sent to the Holy See, unless according to the provisions of the canon under discussion. This provision is merely a specific application of Canon 204, §2; hence, if an Ordinary would make use of such a faculty without the grave and urgent cause required, his action would be illicit, but valid.

The present canon refers only to the exercise of voluntary jurisdiction by an inferior during the actual period of recourse to the Superior. If the latter has received the petition and actually denied the favor, other dispositions must be observed. Thus, the Vicar General cannot validly grant a favor, if the same has been denied by the Bishop, unless indeed the Bishop now consents.[45] Likewise, a favor denied by a Sacred Congregation or Office is invalidly granted by any other Congregation, Office or local Ordinary without the assent of the Congregation or Office which first denied the favor; from which rule the Sacred Penitentiary is exempt since it is exclusively competent directly over the internal forum.[46]

[45] Can. 44, §2.

[46] Can. 43.

Article III—The Exercise of Multiple Delegation

The passive subject of delegation may be one or many; in the latter case delegation may be called *multiple* or *plural*. These many delegates may receive their mandate at different times; it is then said to be *successive*. Or they may all receive it at the same time, in which case it is *simultaneous*. Simultaneous delegation may so be given that each and every delegate is equally competent to execute by himself the mandate; it is then called *solidal (in solidum facta)*. On the other hand, delegation may so be granted that all the delegates must act as a unit in executing the mandate; it is then *collegiate* delegation. These distinctions are essential for an understanding of Canons 205-206.

The legislator first proposes a presumption to establish certitude when there is doubt whether delegation has been granted as solidal or collegiate:

Can. 205, §1. **Si plures iurisdictionem delegatam obtinuerint pro eodem negotio, et dubitetur utrum delegatio facta fuerit in solidum an collegialiter, praesumitur facta in solidum in re voluntaria, collegialiter in re iudiciali.**

Voluntary jurisdiction is presumed solidal, judicial jurisdiction is presumed collegiate; this is merely a presumption, and so yields to the truth, if the contrary is established to be the intention of the delegator. The legislator has aptly induced this distinction, for voluntary power is more efficiently exercised by one than by many, while justice is more securely rendered by many joined in a moral union.[47]

§1. *The Use of Simultaneous Delegation*

In two paragraphs the legislator treats of the exercise of simultaneous delegation:

Can. 205, §2. **Pluribus in solidum delegatis, qui antea negotium occupavit, alios ab eodem excludit, nisi aut posthac impediatur aut nolit ulterius in negotio procedere.**

§3. **Pluribus collegialiter delegatis, omnes simul pro**

[47] C. 21, X, *de officio et potestate iudicis delegati*, I, 29.

actorum validitate in negotio expediendo procedere debent, nisi in mandato aliud cautum sit.

The second paragraph is concerned with solidal delegation. When one of many solidal delegates has once begun to act in the matter for which the mandate was given, all other delegates who have been commissioned, are prevented from acting. Their jurisdiction is not extinguished but is suspended. Hence, if he who has first acted, later becomes impeded, or willingly quits the task, all others again are competent to act. In this case, the same process must be repeated; that is, the delegate who first applies himself to execution of the mandate, after a previous solidal delegate has withdrawn or been impeded, effectively prevents the remaining solidal delegates from exercising their power in the same matter. This principle is an application of the rule, *In re communi potior est conditio prohibentis.*[48] The fact that the delegate in possession is unable or unwilling to proceed in the affair which he has once begun, must be established authentically, by messenger, letter, or witnesses, before the suspension of power in the remaining delegates is removed.[49]

The third paragraph speaks of collegiate delegation. Such delegates are obliged under the penalty of invalidity of the acts to proceed together as a moral unit in executing the matter for which they were delegated. This does not mean that their decisions must be unanimous; the majority vote of the entire body suffices.[50] The canon permits the delegator to provide contrary to the general principle here stated, so that by such arrangement some of the delegates may execute the mandate, even if all are not able to participate.

In judicial matters the diocesan tribunal must proceed as a collegiate unit (*collegialiter*). This does not mean that the acts of the tribunal would be invalid if every judge was not present for each and every act. They must proceed as a unit in rendering sentence under the penalty of nullity.[51] It is not clear that invalidity could be alleged if some of the judges were absent from the acts that precede sentence. Since an ecclesiastical trial is essentially a *written process,* it would suffice if the absent

[48] Reg. 56, R. J., in VI.
[49] Lega, *De Judiciis Ecclesiasticis,* n. 79.
[50] Can. 1577, §1.
[51] Can. 1892.

judges acquainted themselves with the case from the documents before rendering sentence. The examination of witnesses is valid, although the Defender of the Bond is absent, as long as he was cited;[52] he then forms his opinion from the written acts.

Certainly, the tribunal acts as a collegiate unit when it enlists the aid of the Auditor. The latter, if so commissioned, may licitly execute every act of the process as far as the definitive sentence, although the judges of the tribunal are not present.[53]

§2. *The Use of Successive Delegation*

The legislator has thus disposed concerning many delegates who have received their commission at different times:

Can. 206. **Pluribus successive delegatis, ille negotium expedire debet cuius mandatum anterius est nec posteriore rescripto expresse abrogatum fuit.**

This rule is an application of the principle, *Qui prior est tempore, potior est iure.*[54] He whose mandate was first given, obtains possession of the right to proceed, unless his commission has been revoked by a later rescript.

This canon does not solve a difficulty which can arise when it is not possible to determine which of many delegates first received his power. It would seem necessary in such a case to recur to the general canons on rescripts, where it is determined that in such a case, if it is moreover impossible to determine who first sought the disputed faculty, the rescripts of all the conflicting persons are invalid, and recourse must be made to the competent Superior.[55]

---

[52] Can. 1587, §2.
[53] Can. 1582; cf. Noval, *De Processibus*, n. 126.
[54] Reg. 54, R. J., in VI.
[55] Can. 48, §3.

CHAPTER VIII

The Cessation of Delegation

The legislator has determined carefully the manners in which delegated power may have its inception; with no less care has he determined the methods by which it may cease to be. In Canon 207 he first attends to the expiration of all delegation in general; he then gives his attention to the specific problem of collegiate delegation in so far as such delegation may end in an additional manner peculiar to itself.

Article I—The Expiration of Delegation in General

There are many causes which can bring about the extinction of delegated power. These causes can arise either from the mandate itself; or from the part of the active subject or delegator; or from the part of the passive subject or the delegate, as the following canon prescribes:

Can. 207, §1. **Potestas delegata extinguitur, expleto mandato; elapso tempore aut exhausto numero casuum pro quo concessa fuit; cessante causa finali delegationis; revocatione delegantis delegato directe intimata aut renuntiatione delegati deleganti directe intimata et ab eodem acceptata; non autem resoluto iure delegantis, nisi in duobus casibus de quibus in can. 61.**

§1. Cessation Arising from the Mandate Itself

On the part of the mandate, the following causes may end delegation:

(a) The fulfillment of the task for which the mandate was issued; (b) the expiration of the time for which the mandate was given; (c) the completing of the number of cases for which it was granted; (d) the cessation of the final cause for which it was conceded. A brief comment will be made on these several causes.

(a) *Expleto mandato:* When the delegate has brought to a

valid execution his mandate, his power has run its course; this is clear. When he has invalidly executed his mandate, there is reason to doubt whether the power of the delegate always ceases. The Decretals [1] ruled that a delegated judge lost his power whether he executed his mandate laudably or poorly. Authors attempted to read into this law certain exceptions and limitations.[2] In general, however, it was regarded as a general rule that all delegation ended when the mandate was executed even invalidly.[3]

In the present legislation Canon 59, §1, must be considered. This canon states that the executor of a rescript who has in any way erred in executing the same, may again resume the execution of the same rescript. Maroto [4] attempts to restrict this faculty when he declares that if the mandate, morally speaking, is regarded as fulfilled, the delegate cannot reassume his task without a new delegation. This interpretation does violence to Canon 59, §1, which is most ample in its terms; it states that if the executor erred in any way at all (*quoquo modo*), and indeed in the very execution of the rescript (*in rescriptorum executione*), he is free to reenact the execution of the same. There is no reason to believe that the executor may not do the same even if an attempt is morally, or otherwise, complete.

In view of Canon 59, §1, authors generally admit that in voluntary jurisdiction the mandate is not fulfilled unless the execution is valid. When it is question of judicial power, the contrary is maintained by many writers.[5] Noval [6] denies to a judge delegated for one case the right to correct an invalid sentence, but concedes to the judge universally delegated such a faculty, following in this the interpretation of the old law given by Schmalzgrueber.[7] Vidal [8] is more severe and excludes every delegated judge from this privilege.

What, then, is to be said of the delegated judge? May he

---

[1] C. 9, *de officio et potestate iudicis delegati,* I, 29.

[2] Cf. Ojetti, *Commentarium,* I, 266.

[3] D'Annibale, *Summula Theologiae Moralis,* I, n. 77, not. 57.

[4] *Institutiones,* I, 856, not. 3.

[5] Cf. Maroto, *op. cit.,* I, n. 715; Cocchi, *Commentarium,* II, n. 128; Ayrinhac, *General Legislation in the New Code of Canon Law,* p. 366.

[6] *De Processibus,* n. 660.

[7] Lib. I, tit. XXIX, n. 40.

[8] Wernz-Vidal, *Jus Canonicum,* VI, n. 618.

again apply himself to the execution of his mandate, if he has already pronounced a sentence that is invalid? Notwithstanding the opinion of many authors to the contrary, it is reasonable to conclude that such a judge has not fulfilled his mandate by issuing an invalid sentence and that he may, therefore, reassume the process in order to bring it to a valid end.

There is reference here to an *invalid* sentence, not to an *unjust* sentence. A sentence is only then *just* when it renders to the litigants justice; a sentence is *valid* when it does not labor under any of the defects which according to law import invalidity.[9] Hence, a sentence may be just, yet invalid; valid, yet unjust. Against an unjust sentence, the remedy is appeal; against an invalid sentence, the remedy is a complaint of nullity (*querela nullitatis*).[10] It is in this latter case that the judge who has pronounced sentence is competent to review the matter.

In behalf of the opinion which contends the delegated judge is competent to receive the complaint of nullity, the following reasons may be alleged:

1. Canons 1893 and 1895 state that the complaint may be proposed before the judge who has passed the sentence. These canons make no distinction. Hence, the delegated judge is not to be excluded.

2. Since Canon 59, §1, imports a departure from old law at least with regard to voluntary jurisdiction, there is no reason why the same departure should be abhorred in matters of judicial jurisdiction.

3. Canon 1878, §1, permits a judge to correct certain material errors found in the sentence; but authors do not exclude the delegated judge from this right. Therefore, neither should he be excluded from reviewing the processual defects mentioned in Canon 1894, against which the complaint of nullity is proposed.

4. Since the complaint is possible only against an invalid sentence, not against an unjust sentence,[11] and since this invalidity is due entirely to extrinsic, arbitrary causes that can expeditiously be remedied, it is quite plausible that the legislator should desire the same judge to review the case, whether he be ordinary or delegated.

---

[9] Can. 1892; 1894.

[10] Can. 1895.

[11] Wernz-Vidal, *op. cit.*, VI, n. 614.

5. Finally, this opinion is not destitute of extrinsic value, since Creusen [12] and Kinane [13] expressly teach it, while Ojetti [14] implies that the new law has extended the right of iterated execution of a mandate also to judicial power.

It may, therefore, be concluded that in any case the mandate is only then fulfilled when it has been brought to a valid conclusion; to do something invalidly is equivalent to doing nothing at all.

(b) *Elapso tempore:* If the mandate is conceded for a definite period of time, the delegation will end when that period has ceased to be. The time is to be computed according to Canons 32-34. If the time elapses while a particular matter is being executed, that matter may be brought to its juridical conclusion.[15] A mandate granted *ad beneplacitum nostrum* expires with the death of the delegator; this is not so, if it is granted *ad beneplacitum Sedis* or *ad beneplacitum Ordinarii.* Sanchez [16] regards the form, *ad beneplacitum Papae, Episcopi, etc.,* as referring to the dignity, so that it would not end with the death of the incumbent of the office. If it is given *donec revocavero,* it does not cease with the death of the delegator, but requires an explicit act of revocation.

(c) *Exhausto numero casuum:* Delegation, granted for a certain number of cases, ends when the delegate has validly acted the specified number of times. If, however, through inadvertence, he continues to use power granted for the internal forum, his acts will be valid by virtue of Canon 207, §2; which canon must be applied in the same way to the delegate who acts after the time period has elapsed.

(d) *Cessante causa finali delegationis:* From the very nature of delegation, the mandate perishes when the final cause for which it was granted, totally ceases.

§2. *Cessation Arising from the Part of the Delegate*

Renuntiatione delegati deleganti directe intimata et ab eodem acceptata: It is not enough that the delegate renounce his power

[12] Vermeersch-Creusen, *Epitome,* III, n. 242, 4.
[13] "Jurisdiction in the New Code", *IER,* XIII (1919), 216.
[14] *Commentarium,* I, 266.
[15] Ballerini-Palmieri, *Theologia Moralis,* V, 294.
[16] *De Sancto Matrimonii Sacramento,* VIII, D. 28, n. 62.

for delegation to expire; the renunciation must be made known directly to the delegator and it must be accepted by him. It is intimated to him directly, when the knowledge has come from the delegate personally or through his letter or messenger. If the delegator refuses to accept, the delegation still endures.

The Code does not say that delegation ends with the death of the delegate. Nevertheless, it does, unless the delegation was *real,* that is, committed to the person in view of his office or dignity.

§3. *Cessation Arising from the Part of the Delegator*

(a) *Revocatione delegantis delegato directe intimata:* Reiffenstuel[17] taught that the delegator could so recall the mandate that all acts of the delegate from that moment forward would be invalid, whether he acted conscious of the defect or in ignorance of it. The Code requires that the revocation be directly made known to the delegate; hence, the recall does not take effect until the delegate is apprised of the same. It is to be noted that the ordinary Superior, as well as the universal delegate, may recall his mandate at any time. On the other hand, the particular delegate who has legitimately subdelegated the power given to him for a particular case, cannot recall his power, once the subdelegate has begun to act.[18] He may, however, recall his mandate, if he has retained to himself some portion of the power originally committed to him, since in this case he has not abdicated.[19]

(b) *Non autem resoluto iure delegantis nisi in duobus casibus de quibus in can. 61:* If the power of the active subject or delegator ceases for any reason, the power of the delegate does not consequently expire, as a general rule. The delegator may lose his power by natural or civil death, as Schmalzgrueber[20] aptly terms any legal loss of office or power.

The Code makes two exceptions to this rule. First, if the mandate so provides, the delegation will end with the death, civil or natural, of the delegator, unless the matter is no longer

---

[17] Lib. I, tit. XXIX, n. 42.
[18] Schmalzgrueber, lib. I, tit. XXIX, n. 45.
[19] Maroto, *Institutiones,* I, n. 713.
[20] Lib. I, tit. XXIX, n. 48.

intact. Secondly, with the cessation of the right of the Superior delegation also expires, if the mandate contains a favor to be granted (*gratia facienda*) by the delegate to persons named therein, and the matter is no longer integral.

The present canon mentions these two exceptions explicitly. A third exception, however, must be induced. Canon 1725, n. 3, states as follows: *Cum citatio legitime peracta fuerit aut partes sponte in iudicium venerint. . . . In iudice delegato firma redditur iurisdictio ita ut non expiret resoluto iure delegantis.* Wherefore, only then is judicial jurisdiction rendered so fixed as not to expire with the cessation of the right of the delegator, when legitimate citation or its equivalent has taken place. Therefore, it is necessary to conclude that *before* citation or its equivalent has taken place, delegated judicial power ends with the termination of the right of the Superior.

Is not this interpretation contrary to the present canon which expressly admits of only *two* exceptions? That seems to be so. Hence, the Code has caused a doubt, for the solution of which one must recur to the old law. Wernz,[21] commenting on pre-Code law, makes precisely the distinctions exposed above, so that his doctrine is conformable entirely to the three exceptions, rather than the two. Moreover, the old authors,[22] in treating of the delegated judge, stated that the death of the delegator implied the cessation of power in the delegate. Therefore, it is in keeping with the old law to include the exception of judicial power, and it is in harmony with the new law, since otherwise Canon 1725, n. 3, would be without meaning.

Maroto [23] states that the power of the delegate is suspended when the delegator is affected by the censure of suspension. This is not true; since delegation does not regularly expire, except in the case of judicial delegation, with the total cessation of the right of the delegator, surely it is not affected by the censure inflicted upon him.[24]

---

[21] II, n. 561, III.

[22] Santi, lib. I, tit. XXIX, n. 34; Bouix, *De Judiciis Ecclesiasticis,* I, 160; Schmalzgrueber, lib. I, tit. XXIX, n. 48; Reiffenstuel, lib. I, tit. XXIX, n. 129.

[23] *Institutiones,* n. 715.

[24] Chelodi, *Jus de Personis,* n. 129.

Article II—The Cessation of Collegiate Delegation

Collegiate delegation, which implies a moral union of several delegates, so expires:

Can. 207, §3. **Pluribus collegialiter delegatis, si unus deficiat, aliorum quoque delegatio expirat, nisi aliud ex tenore delegationis constet.**

If one of many collegiate delegates loses his power for any reason, the power of all fellow-delegates likewise is extinguished, unless the mandate has provided otherwise.

Authors suggest other exceptions to this rule. If a delegate whose power is now about to expire, subdelegates another, the collegiate body does not cease.[25] This, however, must be understood in accordance with the general principles of delegation; hence, a particular delegate, empowered by a prelate inferior to the Pope, may not subdelegate.[26] It is likewise suggested that the power of the group does not cease, if the matter is no longer integral.[27] This latter must be accepted with caution. Certain processes are irreparably invalid if sentence has been passed by an insufficient number of judges.[28] Hence, in such a case the cessation of power in one delegate will affect the validity of the process, unless more than a sufficient number of judges was convened.

Article III—Acts Placed with Inadvertence

Inadvertence is actual forgetfulness or failure of memory. When power has been granted for a certain period of time or for a certain number of cases, it is only human to forget when the limit has been attained. To succor those who in the internal forum might be injured by such a human defect, the legislator has provided this new law:

Can. 207, §2. **Sed potestate pro foro interno concessa,**

---

[25] Wernz, II, n. 561, II; Maroto, *Institutiones,* I, n. 715.

[26] Can. 199, §4.

[27] Wernz, *loc. cit.;* Cocchi, *Commentarium,* II, n. 129; Wernz-Vidal, *Jus Canonicum,* II, 370, not. 40.

[28] Can. 1892, n. 1; 1576, §1.

actus per inadvertentiam positus, elapso tempore vel exhausto casuum numero, validus est.

By this law the Church supplies jurisdiction of the internal forum in the circumstances mentioned. The principle is applicable to both sacramental and extrasacramental forum, since the legislator has not distinguished.

CHAPTER IX

Supplied Jurisdiction

Barbarius was a slave who so effectively concealed his lowly origin, that the discriminating Roman people elevated him to the dignity of Praetor. In this capacity, Barbarius handed down many judicial sentences. Since, however, a slave was not a fit subject for jurisdiction, the official acts of Barbarius were invalid. A series of invalid acts which affect the public interest, can cause havoc in a community. Hence, to avert such evil consequences, the Roman people resolved that the invalid acts of Barbarius should be ratified, as though they were valid from the beginning. This solution, they said, was a more human method of acting; and, after all, imperial Rome could have given jurisdiction even to a slave, had she so wished.[1] This decision of the Roman people was the foundation of a juridical principle that has been acknowledged by all posterity.

The Romans, well pleased with the solution that they had found for a difficult problem, extended the principle to other matters. The *Senatusconsultum Macedonianum* made invalid all loans of money which a *filiusfamilias* might negotiate; but the Digests [2] ruled that if the borrower was commonly regarded as a *paterfamilias*, though he was not, he would no longer be protected by the immunity of the former provision. Hence, the common opinion of people brought about the validity of what was in itself invalid. An extension, somewhat similar, was made in the case of the public notaries (*tabelliones*).[3]

Pope Lucius III [4] ordained that defects in ecclesiastical law should be supplied by the provisions of civil law. Thus indirectly the law *Barbarius* was canonized. Innocent III [5] made use of the principle when he declared invalid the sentences pro-

[1] Fr. 3, D. 1, 14.
[2] Fr. 3, D. 14, 6.
[3] Nov. 44, 1, §1-4.
[4] C. 1, X, *de novi operis nuntiatione,* V, 32.
[5] C. 24, X, *de sententia et re iudicata,* II, 27.

nounced by a judge who had been *publicly* excommunicated. Since in that era all excommunication deprived the delinquent of jurisdiction, it is clear that jurisdiction could be supplied for a sentence pronounced by an occultly excommunicated judge. The Decree of Gratian more explicitly refers to the principle in words most similar to the Roman law.[6]

Out of these vestiges canonists and theologians deduced a general principle. On March 10, 1770, the Sacred Congregation of the Council made use of it, and declared valid a marriage, otherwise invalid, because the common opinion of the faithful regarded the assisting priest as pastor.[7] The same principle, together with extensions of the law, has been incorporated into the Code in the following terms:

***Can. 209.* In errore communi aut in dubio positivo et probabili sive iuris sive facti, iurisdictionem supplet Ecclesia pro foro tum externo tum interno.**

Article I—The Concept of Supplied Jurisdiction

Certain juridical acts can be validly placed only by those equipped with authority. Although an unauthorized agent might observe every formality required by the law, his act will be invalid. It will escape no one that a series of invalid acts, placed by an unauthorized agent, maliciously or in good faith, especially when such acts are distributed throughout a long period of time, will work havoc in society. It is a function, then, of good government to provide against this peril, not indeed in the sense that all acts of themselves invalid must be rendered valid, for thus the legislator would contradict himself, but in the sense that the legislator provides for those cases in which a general danger to souls is verified.[8] The Church so provides by *supplying* jurisdiction to an agent who lacks it. This supplied power is conceived as a delegation *a iure;* [9] the active subject of this extraordinary delegation is the common

[6] "Si servus, dum putaretur liber, ex delegatione sententiam dixit, quamvis postea, in servitutem delapsus sit, sententia ab eo dicta rei iudicatae firmitatem tenet."—C. 1, C. III, q. 7.

[7] Richter, *Canones et Decreta Concilii Tridentini,* p. 229, n. 51.

[8] Suarez, D. XXVI, sec. 6, n. 7.

[9] Lehmkuhl, *Theologia Moralis,* II, n. 387

law, in the sense that the Author of that law so disposes.[10] The power is given, not habitually, but *in actu;* the agent does not possess the power before he uses it, nor does he retain it afterwards. He possesses it only as long as is necessary for the valid exercise of the act.[11]

The Church supplies only those things which pertain to the *state and condition of persons.*[12] Hence, the omission of formalities required by law for the validity of acts, is not supplied for by the Church. Thus, supplied jurisdiction may make valid the absolutions of a putative confessor; but if a competent confessor should hear the confession of religious women outside the legitimate place for confession, his acts will be invalid and the Church will not supply.[13]

The Church can supply only that power, the disposition of which is entrusted to her; she cannot, therefore, supply what is required by divine or natural law.[14] She cannot, consequently, supply confessional jurisdiction to an agent who is not a priest, nor to an agent destitute of the use of reason, nor to a competent agent, simulating absolution. Sanchez[15] maintained that if a baptized male should invalidly be elected Pope, the Church could supply jurisdiction so that all his jurisdictional acts, that do not presuppose the power of orders, would be valid, since divine law requires no more than that the subject of ecclesiastical jurisdiction be a baptized male.

It was once disputed whether the Church could supply jurisdiction of the internal forum. Sanchez[16] and Pontius[17] met this difficulty and responded affirmatively. The present canon explicitly asserts that the Church supplies in both internal and external forum.

---

[10] Cappello, *De Sacramentis,* II, n. 486.

[11] Lehmkuhl, *Casus Conscientiae,* II, n. 429; Wernz-Vidal, *Jus Canonicum,* II, 368.

[12] D'Annibale, *Summula Theologiae Moralis,* I, n. 79, not. 75.

[13] Cf. Pont. Comm. ad CC. Auth. Interp., 28 Dec. 1927—*AAS,* XX (1928), 61.

[14] Pontius, *De Sacramento Matrimonii,* V, cap. 19, n. 5; De Lugo, *De Justitia et Jure,* Dis. XXXVII, sec. 3, n. 25; Billuart, *De Justitia et Jure, Dis.* XII, art. 1, p. 3; Ferraris, *Prompta Bibliotheca,* v. *Confessarius,* n. 36 ss.

[15] *De Sancto Matrimonii Sacramento,* III, D. 22, n. 28.

[16] *Op. cit.,* III, D. 22, n. 12 ss.

[17] *Op. cit.,* V, cap. 19, n. 8.

By positive disposition of law it is determined that the Church will supply jurisdiction in two cases; namely, *in common error, and in positive and probable doubt of law and of fact.* The following two articles will treat respectively of these circumstances.

Article II—Common Error

Few canons of the Code have provoked such controversy as the canon under discussion. It would seem as though authors had determined to make complex what the legislator determined to make simple. The codification of canon law was a sincere effort to simplify law; opportune changes were made and clearly indicated in the new law. On the whole, however, the Code is a collection of old laws. The legislator has made sacred the old law and the interpretation attached to it by the classical authors.[18] Wherefore, in doubt concerning the meaning of the new law, the old law prevails. This same principle is applicable to Canon 209, as well as to the entire codification.

§1. *The Traditional Interpretation*

The common opinion of pre-Code writers was that the Church supplied when with common error a *colored title (titulus coloratus)* was verified; yet many eminent authors, such as Pontius, Joannes Andreas, and Hostiensis,[19] did not require the colored title. St. Alphonsus [20] regarded the latter opinion as solidly probable. It is to be noted that the term *titulus coloratus* had a very definite and restricted meaning. The colored title was a *title actually conferred by a legitimate superior, competent to confer it, but invalidly.* It was thus distinguished from a merely *putative* or *fictitious* title, which was present whenever a person pretended to be endowed with power, whether in good or bad faith, as long as the pretense was not based on the act of a legitimate Superior.[21] Thus, Sanchez [22] proposes the case in

[18] Can. 6.

[19] Cf. Ferraris, *Prompta Bibliotheca* v. *Confessarius*, n. 38 ss.

[20] V, n. 572.

[21] D'Annibale, *Summula Theologiae Moralis,* I, n. 79, not. 73; Benedict XIV, *Casus Conscientiae,* IV, 515; Sporer, *Theologia Moralis,* III, n. 374; Scavini, *Theologia Moralis,* III, n. 374; Ballerini-Palmieri, *Theologia Moralis,* V, n. 636; Gury, *Theologia Moralis,* II, n. 548.

[22] *De Sancto Matrimonii Sacramento,* III, D. 22, n. 63.

which a Municipal Council appointed a pastor, who then exercised the duties of his office for two years; this pastor, although commonly accepted as such by the faithful, did not enjoy a *colored title,* since the title to the office did not derive from a Superior competent to bestow the same. Lehmkuhl [23] similarly indicates that credentials, falsified by a priest, are not a colored title, since such have not proceeded from the legitimate ecclesiastical Superior.

When the Code, therefore, by a significant silence suppressed the need of a colored title, it merely determined that a colored title, accepted in its specific sense, is no longer required. No more than this can be deduced. The Code demands common error and does not care from what sources this error arises. Nevertheless, the words of Billuart,[24] who did not require the colored title, still ring true, since he stated that common error is scarcely conceivable without some *apparent* title.

It is to be noted that the authors distinguished well between the title and common error. The two are distinct concepts, one of which could be verified without the presence of the other. All required common error; some required also the colored title. But even those who rejected the necessity of a colored title, demanded some foundation for error, since error in a multitude cannot arise without something sensible to produce it. The intellect conceives only what the senses perceive.

The Code has accepted the terminology of the authors, insisting upon *common error.* What, then, is common error? The old writers understood by this term precisely what the words convey. First, it is an error; that is, a false judgment or misapprehension. Secondly, this error must be common; that is, shared by many. The object of such an error must be the personal qualifications of an agent, who is, therefore, believed to possess powers that he actually lacks. The authors insisted that many actually participate in the error; hence, the error of a few is particular, and not common, and the Church will not supply.[25] It was regarded as sufficient if the error was

[23] *Casus Conscientiae,* II, n. 433; cf. De Lugo, *De Justitia et Jure,* Dis. 37, n. 21.

[24] *De Poenitentia,* D. VI, art. 4, §1.

[25] Pontius, *op. cit.,* V, cap. 19, n. 4; Billuart, *op. cit.,* Dis. VI, art. 4, §1; Reiffenstuel, lib. IV, tit. III, n. 76; Ferraris, *op. cit.,* v. *Jurisdictio,* n. 32; Scavini, *Theologia Moralis,* III, n. 374.

common in the particular place in which the agent was acting, although elsewhere the defect in that same agent might be common knowledge. Sanchez [26] illustrates this from the case of Barbarius, whose servile condition was undoubtedly well known in the place whence he fled. Finally, the place in which common error may be verified is any collective unit, as a diocese, parish, or religious community. Reiffenstuel [27] admitted that a common opinion could exist among a community of ten or more persons.

Among the authors the greatest discrepancy will be found with regard to the number who must be in error in order that such error might be called common. Many authors do not discuss the question; hence, it is evident that they did not understand the term in any abnormal sense, which would always demand elucidation. The majority of the writers required that all or nearly all, of the community should participate in the error;[28] hence, they stated that if a few should know of the defect, the error would continue to be common. Gennari [29] more recently contended that common error was verified if the *majority* of the community was in error. This opinion is sustained by the Digests [30] in which the immunity of the *Senatusconsultum* was denied to a minor who commonly was regarded as a *paterfamilias*; the expression used is, *quia plerisque videbatur*. Lehmkuhl [31] believed that the error of *many* was sufficient to constitute common error. This controversy, therefore, constitutes a doubt of law; hence, the more favorable interpretation may be followed and the Church will supply jurisdiction at least in virtue of this doubt. In any of the interpretations given error will be actually common.

Common error is the false judgment of many. This need not be *practical* error; *speculative* error suffices. It is not a question of how many have approached a particular agent, but how many believe him to be endowed with jurisdiction. Hence,

---

[26] *De Sancto Matrimonii Sacramento,* III, D. 22, n. 9.

[27] Lib. V, tit. 1, n. 249.

[28] Reiffenstuel, lib. IV, tit. III, n. 76; Schmalzgrueber, lib. IV, tit. III, n. 22; Billuart, *De Poenitentia,* Dis. VI, art. 4. §1; Scavini, *Theologia Moralis,* III, n. 374; Sporer, *Theologia Moralis,* III, n. 714.

[29] *Consultationes Morales,* 69.

[30] Fr. 3, D. 14, 6.

[31] *Theologia Moralis,* II, n. 389.

even before one person has approached, the state of common error can exist.[32]

It is to be noted that a condition of common error can exist, although here and now, *in actu secundo,* many of the faithful do not elicit a false judgment. All that is required is that here and now many of the faithful be *in error*; they must labor under a false impression or persuasion; they must be so mentally disposed, that if asked, they would respond that this particular agent is a confessor, a pastor, a judge, or the like. To demand more than this of a community is impossible. Yet, such a state of error constitutes error *de facto*; for in the minds of the faithful who are so deceived, there was once an actual error which still virtually perseveres. Until such a state of mind is corrected, or entirely lost by the lapse of time, the error exists virtually, subconsciously, but really.[33] The elements of an actual false judgment are present in the minds of many who are, therefore, in a state of error. In such a condition the Church will supply jurisdiction.

That such a virtual error, once actual and still persevering, is sufficient, may be substantiated from the sources. It is well to return to Barbarius who, as Praetor, pronounced judicial sentences. Few of a community have occasion to approach an official to obtain ministration of justice; hence, few approached Barbarius for this purpose. When the Roman people validated the worthless acts of the impostor, no question was raised as to how many citizens actually, *in actu secundo,* adverted even to the existence of Barbarius as he sat in the tribunal. It was sufficient that he was commonly known as Praetor. On the day of his elevation to that dignity, all Romans adverted to him and hailed him. He soon was crowded from their minds by the pursuits of the Forum. Yet the Romans were so disposed, that, if asked, they would have assented that Barbarius was Praetor and competent judge. Their actual judgment first elicited, and perhaps occasionally reiterated, persisted virtually, subconsciously, but nevertheless really. Such is common error.

A practical example will better illustrate the notions exposed above. It is announced from the pulpit that Father Stephen

[32] *Lehmkuhl, Theologia Moralis,* II, n. 389.

[33] Jombart, "L'erreur commune," *NRT,* L (1923), 173; Vermeersch, *Theologia Moralis,* III, n. 459.

will hear confessions on the following evening; when the good religious appears, he has failed to obtain jurisdiction. The public announcement has caused the generality of the people to believe that Father Stephen is a confessor; at the moment of the announcement they formed a judgment to this effect, for the human mind is so constituted that it does not rest in a simple apprehension of truth, but necessarily assents, dissents or doubts. On the following evening many will not advert to the confessor; yet, they are so disposed, that, if they are reminded of him, they will agree that a visiting confessor may be found at the parish church.[34] Such error, once actual, now virtual, but *de facto,* is sufficient reason for the Church to supply jurisdiction.

On March 10, 1770, the Sacred Congregation of the Council applied the principle of common error to a matrimonial case. After the death of a certain pastor, a priest assumed the burdens of the parish, among which was the marriage of Anthony and Nicolasia. The Sacred Congregation declared the marriage valid, thus rejecting the decision of a lower tribunal. The evidence showed that a colored title was present; then, an examination of more than thirty witnesses, parishioners selected from different groups and ranks (*ex omni coetu atque ordine decerpti*), revealed that the priest was commonly regarded as the lawful pastor. The Congregation assigned as the reasons for the decision: *non solum opinio in populo, sed titulus quoque colorativus in sacerdote.*[35]

Since this is an authentic decision of the Holy See, it may be regarded as a true norm. Hence, the following deductions, all confirmatory of the doctrine exposed in the preceding pages, will be valuable:

1. The examination of thirty or more witnesses indicates that moral unanimity is not required; the error of many will suffice. However, it must be truly error (*opinio in populo*); pure ignorance is not enough.

2. There was no question as to how many actually approached the putative pastor for ministrations; speculative error was sufficient.

3. There was no question as to how many actually, *in actu*

[34] Vermeersch, *Theologia Moralis,* III, n. 459.

[35] Pallotini, vol. XIII, V. *Matrimonium,* XV, n. 90.

secundo, erred at the time when the ceremony took place. The fact that all were ready to acknowledge the minister as their pastor indicated at least virtual error.

4. Neither the public exercise of parochial functions, nor the colored title, was enough; such facts could be proved by two witnesses. With these facts verified, thirty and more witnesses, selected from different classes, were examined to verify the existence of a false mental state among the parishioners. A mere public fact, therefore, did not constitute common error.

In the preceding pages the authority of the classical authors has been called upon. Their notion of common error has not been changed. Had the Code adopted any other meaning or created any fiction, the legislator in a few words could, and would, have expressed it. Every law of interpretation compels the canonist to adhere to the doctrine exposed above; and as a matter of fact, such is the more common opinion of recent commentators.

§2. *Common Error de Iure*

Recent writers have attempted to depart from the traditional interpretation of common error, in order to eliminate all need of determining the number of persons who must be in error, if this is to be common. The new theory, therefore, does not require actual error, or at least actual common error. Precisely what is does require, is difficult to determine, since authors who propose this opinion, are by no means in accord. It is necessary to examine, not only the principle they state, but also the examples they cite; from the latter it will often appear that authors differ widely from those whom they pretend to follow.

In general the proponents of common error *de iure* require merely a *public foundation* for error, from which many of the community will necessarily be lead into error, if things follow their natural course. Hence, this *common error* is a fiction of law, for it is neither *common,* nor is it *error,* when the Church begins to supply. Yet, it is maintained that this is what the law means by the term, *common error.* Such error was never *actual*; hence, it cannot be conceived as *virtual,* since the virtual is that which was once actual and still perseveres. In this the authors are not consistent. Adloff [36] professes that *virtual* common error suffices; yet, he accepts as an example the case in which the name of a priest is attached to a confessional, although none of the faithful advert to the fact, and he holds that the Church will supply from that moment on. The same writer indicates the great difference existing between this case and the case of a public announcement made to the congregation; yet, he calls both *virtual* error. The example cited by Adloff is not that of virtual error; no error has been made and hence no error exists even virtually. Similarly, Couly [37] speaks of error *virtually* affecting the community, while he cites as an example the priest who merely enters a confessional. Again, no error was ever actual, and no error exists as virtual. Jombart [38] describes as virtual error that which has actually been present in the minds of the faithful, owing to a public announcement, and which still continues to exist obscurely or subconsciously in the mind. Creusen [39] terms *interpretative* error, that which is conceived to exist after the verification of a public foundation for error and before such error has become actual.

In order that the terminology of this paper might be perfectly understood, the following descriptions will be offered. They are based on the divisions of intention, used constantly by moralists:

1. *Interpretative* error is that which has never existed actually; it is merely a fiction. It would now be verified, if conditions were otherwise. It is, therefore, nothing real; it is merely presumed. Thus, a fact, of its nature public, which has never come to the knowledge of a community, is merely interpretative knowledge until such a time as it actually becomes known.

2. *Virtual* error is that which was once actual and now continues to exist at least subconsciously, just as a virtual intention was once actual and continues to exert its influence.

3. Error *de facto* is that error which is either actual or virtual, since virtual error too implies the *fact* of error.

4. Error *de iure* is that which is a fiction of law. It is not

[36] "L'erreur commune et la jurisdiction suppléée," *Bulletin Eccles. du Diocèse de Strasbourg,* XLVI (1927), 254 ss.

[37] "La Jurisdiction Suppléée du Canon 209," *Canoniste Contemporain,* XLVII (1925), 456.

[38] "L'Erreur Commune," *NRT,* L (1923), 174.

[39] Vermeersch-Creusen, *Epitome,* I, n. 284.

factual. Thus, a fact that of its nature would lead many into error is not *common error*; yet, to this phrase the law could attach such a meaning, if the legislator so willed. Such is only interpretative error.

It is the contention of the present writer that at least *virtual common error*—therefore, error *de facto*—is required by Canon 209. Against this opinion Cappello [40] contends vehemently, and with him Vidal,[41] Adloff,[42] and Arquer [43] agree. Damen [44] regards the opinion as probable.

The Code requires *common error* before the Church will supply. In the theory advanced recently no error is required. The authors cited demand merely a fact placed publicly from which many may be led into error. There is no question here of a fiction of law. It is beyond the powers of canonists to create such a fiction. When the Code made use of the traditional expression, the evident intention of the legislator was to make no change; he merely reiterated and confirmed the expression which the Holy See had at least once applied, and which authors throughout the centuries had understood in essentially the same light. Every law of interpretation sustains adherence to the traditional notion of common error. Hence, it is not necessary to disprove the theory of Cappello and others; the burden of proof is theirs. They must prove, not merely that it would be good for the Church to supply in such circumstances, but that the Church actually does so supply. In this the exponents of interpretative error have failed.

In the first place, authors have failed to determine when the foundation for error is *public*. Surely, if it is placed in the presence of *many*, the error will already be common *de facto*. Guns [45] insists that it must be *public*. But when is it such? Is it a public fact because it is placed in a public place, as in a church? Does it matter whether the church be in the heart of a city, or will a deserted, country mission suffice? Is it public merely because it can be proved by two witnesses? Cappello [46]

[40] *De Sacramentis*, II, n. 490.
[41] Wernz-Vidal, *Jus Canonicum*, II, n. 381.
[42] *Loc. cit.*
[43] *El Error Comun*, n. 14 ss.
[44] Aertnys-Damen, *Theologia Moralis*, II, n. 359.
[45] "L'Erreur Commune," *NRT*, L (1923), 540.
[46] *Op. cit.*, II, n. 491.

indicates that the very fact a priest sits in a confessional of a *public* church to which the faithful *may approach* constitutes such a fact. Would he say the same of a semi-public oratory? What, then, is a public fact? It is no easier to determine when a fact is really public than it is to determine when error is really common. The authors have failed to determine precisely when publicity is verified. It is inconceivable that a fact should be public merely because it has come about in a public place, even though such a place actually is deserted. But if many are present, common error *de facto* will be verified; if but a few, the error will be particular and all authors agree in condemning the concept of supplied jurisdiction in particular error; if none are present, merely ignorance, not error, is verified.[47] Hence, the theory is not without difficulty.

Cappello[48] attempts to prove his opinion by five arguments. These will be proposed and answered as follows:

Arg. I. From the very fact that the foundation of error is *public,* error too can reasonably be called *public.*

R.—This argument arbitrarily assumes the very point to be proved. The concept is not sustained by the Code, nor by authors. The fact that a priest sits in the confessional of a public church, independently of how many actually see him, is no indication that the faithful will advert to him. A fact, public by its nature, is only a *possible* cause of error; many circumstances are to be considered before it can be called a *probable* cause. *A posse ad esse non valet illatio.*

Arg. II and III. If error *de iure* is not admitted, it would be necessary to ask how many have erred or are in error.

R.—The Code has provided for this difficulty in the second section of the canon; it is now certain that the Church supplies in doubt of fact. If the priest has a probable reason to believe there is a general false impression among the people, the Church will supply by reason of his doubt.

Arg. IV. It would be necessary to know how many must be in error in order that error might be regarded as common.

R.—It is sufficient that many be in error. There is no need for undue scrupulosity, since the Church supplies in doubt. The

[47] Kelly, *The Jurisdiction of the Confessor,* p. 126.
[48] *Op. cit.,* II, n. 490.

older authors left such judgments to the prudence of the minister.[49]

Arg. V. The legislator wished to end all controversy by Canon 209; hence, he so wished to clarify the matter that from the words of the law there might be no room for doubt and anxiety.

R.—This argument can effectively be retorted. There is no room for doubt. The *words of the law* demand common error! Clearly, the legislator settled three distinct controversies; the Church now supplies (a) without a colored title; (b) in doubt of fact as well as of law; and (c) in both fora. It is to be presumed then, that he settled the controversy begun by Bucceroni.[50] In what way did he settle it? By reiterating the time-honored phrase, *Ecclesia supplet in errore communi.* If the legislator has settled the difficulty, he has done so to the discomfort of those who are content with a mere foundation for error.

Hence, it is to be concluded that the exponents of error *de iure* have not established by juridical argument what they have arbitrarily assumed. On the other hand, the following remarks will indicate that such a theory is not expedient:

1. Any priest could absolve anywhere; it would be sufficient to declare himself prepared to hear confessions.[51] Such a theory would be a peril to the rigid laws, promulgated for the common good, on the need of jurisdiction that is ordinary or delegated *ab homine.* These laws have been made precisely that priests might not enter the sacred tribunal without their Superiors having first judged them competent.

2. The force of invalidating laws would be weakened. If it is a public fact merely to enter a confessional, then it is a public fact to stand at the altar prepared to assist at a marriage, or to sit in the usual tribunal, prepared to pass sentence. Thus, validity would be extended to invalid nuptials and void sentences, since the principle applies to all such matters. Canon 209 must not be regarded as a ubiquitous law, scurrying through the Code to nullify the provisions of invalidating laws. Its application must therefore be restricted.

---

[49] D'Annibale, *Summula Theologiae Moralis,* I, n. 242, not. 49.
[50] *Casus Conscientiae,* 129, n. 5.
[51] Vermeersch, *Theologia Moralis,* III, n. 459.

3. This opinion would require an apparent title, but no error; the Code requires error, and is silent about the title.

4. This interpretation would extend the notion of common error to an abnormal extent, merely to provide for a few unusual circumstances. The Code has provided so that confessors who do not advert to the expiration of their mandate, caused by lapse of time or of number of cases, may continue to absolve validly. It has also provided for the anxiety and doubts of a confessor, by supplying him with jurisdiction in any circumstance of probable doubt. All that remains is the case of the confessor who, without having enjoyed jurisdiction before, believes himself to be endowed with the same, when he is not. Such a case is not more than possible, and makes good discussion for the *Casus Conscientiae*. Practically, however, it is a rare and extraordinary occurrence; for such the good legislator does not provide. The evil consequences of relaxation of ecclesiastical discipline far outweigh the individual hardships of a few.[52]

§3. *Common Ignorance*

Very recently Kelly[53] has introduced a unique explanation of common error. This writer maintains that the Church will supply jurisdiction in *common ignorance,* i. e., as long as the defect of jurisdiction in a particular agent remains occult and commonly unknown. Kelly argues that error and ignorance are convertible terms in law; he sustains this by various citations from the writings of canonists and by a reference to Canon 2202, §3, where the legislator states that what has been said of ignorance applies equally well to error and inadvertence.[54] Moreover, this author does not require any public fact as a foundation; since the Code does not mention the colored title, no title is necessary; to require a public fact would be to demand "something similar to the colored title of old."[55] Hence, he concludes, the Church is always prepared to supply jurisdiction as long as it is commonly unknown that the agent lacks jurisdiction.

---

[52] Suarez, D. 26, sec. 6, n. 7; O'Neill, *IER,* XXI (1923), 300; O'Donnell, *IER*, XVI (1920), 499-502.

[53] *The Jurisdiction of the Confessor,* p. 117 ss.

[54] Kelly, *op. cit.,* p. 129.

[55] *Ibid,* p. 125.

This interpretation is entirely inadmissible. In the first place, the silence of the Code with regard to the need of a colored title does not indicate that a sensible fact is not required as a cause of error. As has been stated before,[56] the colored title had a very specific meaning. The silence of the legislator merely indicates that no *colored* title is required. The legislator is not concerned with the cause of common error; if common error is present, regardless of how it has arisen, the Church will supply.[57] But knowledge, true or false, is inconceivable without sense perception; the mind conceives what the senses perceive. There is no more similarity between a colored title and a public fact than there is between any two sensible objects. The Code suppressed by silence the controversy which questioned whether a *colored* title was required rather than an imagined, putative or any other title. The silence of the Code settles that question and no more.

Are error and ignorance convertible terms? As ancient an author as Menochio[58] decried the confusing of these terms. Error is a false judgment; it is a positive act of the mind by which something is misapprehended. Ignorance, however, implies no act of cognition; it is a lack of knowledge.[59] Since error is defective knowledge, it presupposes ignorance. Ignorance, however, can very well be conceived without error. Thus, an infidel to whom the Gospel has not yet been preached is in ignorance of Christ, not in error concerning Him, since no judgment has been made.[60] Error adds to ignorance a false judgment.[61] In a word, ignorance is nothing, while error is something.

Kelly has accepted ignorance in this totally negative sense and made it convertible with error. In this he fails, for the authors cited by him have not so accepted ignorance. These authors speak of ignorance as affecting human acts.[62] But, as

[56] Cf. supra, p. 122.

[57] Cappello, *De Sacramentis,* II, n. 496.

[58] *De Praesumptionibus,* VI, p. XXIII, n. 2 ss.

[59] St. Thomas, 4 sent., dist. 30, art. 1; Ryan, *An Introduction to Philosophy,* p. 235; Walsh, *Tractatus de Actibus Humanis,* n. 214; Waffelaert, *De Dubio Solvendo in Re Morali,* n. 109.

[60] Walsh, *op. cit.,* n. 215.

[61] Cappello, *op. cit.,* III, n. 583.

[62] V. g., Cappello, *op. cit.,* II, n. 529. "Ignorantia . . . hic sumitur . . . prout nempe in actiones humanas *actualiter* influit."

Kelly admits,[63] *ignorance in action is error.* Ignorance, as a negative concept, cannot influence or cause an act; a negative cause is an absurdity. When, however, an agent places an act, which he would not place if he were cognizant of certain facts, he has acted in ignorance and has, therefore, erred. Only in this condition are ignorance and error convertible. Hence, the authors quoted by Kelly can be understood only with regard to ignorance that has occasioned a false judgment or action, not with regard to inert, negative ignorance. This is so true that the very passages cited by Kelly deal for the most part with *defects that vitiate the human act.*[64] The authors, therefore, do not militate in Kelly's ranks.

The same may be said of the argument drawn from Canon 2202, §3, for here too there is question of ignorance in action, since a violation of a law may be an act. If, however, the violation is an omission, due to ignorance of law, it cannot properly be said to be error, but merely ignorance. Moreover, if an argument is to be deduced from this canon, Kelly must conclude that inadvertence too is convertible with error. But Canon 207, §2, provides for the supply of jurisdiction in inadvertence. Why this explicit provision, if it is included in Canon 209?

Kelly attempts to deduce an argument from the law *Barbarius.* He states that while Barbarius was acting as Praetor, nothing but "general ignorance of the defective power of the official existed among the people." [65] This is not true. The Roman people not only were ignorant of the servile condition of Barbarius, but at the same time they positively *believed* him to be a freeman and their Praetor. This is confirmed by the Decree of Gratian.[66]

The repugnance of the opinion proposed is all the more evident from the consequences that must follow therefrom. If one admits that the Church will always supply unless the defect of the agent is commonly known, the following would result:

1. Any priest, travelling outside his diocese in a place where

[63] *Op. cit.,* p. 129.

[64] Can. 104; Badii, *Institutiones,* I, n. 87; Vermeersch-Creusen, *Epitome,* I, n. 197; Maroto, *Institutiones,* I, n. 402; Wernz-Vidal, *Jus Canonicum,* II, n. 39.

[65] *Op. cit.,* p. 130.

[66] "Servus, dum *putaretur* liber . . ." C. 1, C. III, q. 7.

even his presence is commonly unknown, could validly absolve any penitent. Moreover, he could do the same even if he and the penitent adverted to the lack of jurisdiction, since the ignorance would still be common.

2. Any layman could validly assist at any marriage, since people would scarcely advert to his lack of authority; and authors generally have admitted that the clerical state is not required for assistance at matrimony, except by ecclesiastical law.

3. Any cleric, whose presence was not adverted to in a particular community, could validly dispense *even himself* from the most serious ecclesiastical laws, since to do so is an act of jurisdiction.

What logically leads to absurd conclusions is in itself absurd.

§4. *Common Error Applied to Delegation*

There can be no doubt that the principle of supplied jurisdiction in common error is applicable to delegated jurisdiction. This is established by Canon 1606 which states that the principle is to be applied to delegated judges. It is not so certain, however, that the same principle may be applied to one who is delegated invalidly for one, particular act. Jombart [67] persuaded by the words of Reiffenstuel [68] has come to the conclusion that the Church will not supply in such a case, since the law considers only those matters which can cause damage to the common good. To this Vermeersch [69] also agrees.

The present writer would not deny this conclusion. Yet, the following remarks may be pertinent. First, if the community is actually of the opinion that a certain priest is competent to assist at a particular marriage, the error would then be common although its object would be particular. The Code requires only common error. Secondly, many old authors applied the principle to the particular delegate. Thus, Pontius [70] applied it, appealing to the old formula, "Si servus, dum putaretur liber, ex *delegatione* sententiam dixit . . ." [71] Sanchez,[72] too, applies

[67] "L'erreur Commune," *NRT,* L (1923), 363-5.

[68] Lib. IV, tit. III, n. 76.

[69] *Theologia Moralis,* III, n. 799.

[70] *De Sacramento Matrimonii,* V, cap. 19, n. 11.

[71] C. 1, C. III, q. 7.

[72] *De Sancto Matrimonii Sacramento,* III, D. 22, n. 61.

the principle to a layman, delegated for a marriage, and commonly regarded as a priest. D'Annibale [73] states that a deacon delegated for a marriage will invalidly assist, unless he is believed commonly to be a priest. DeLugo [74] applies the principle to the delegate, without distinguishing between the universal and particular delegate.

Hence, in the rare instance in which common error actually will be verified concerning a particular delegate, it is probable that the Church will supply.

§5. *Conclusion*

In the preceding pages the traditional notion of common error has been defended. The legislator has in no way insinuated that any departure therefrom is to be countenanced. If any doubt remains, the general policy of the legislator must be applied: *In dubio . . . a veteri iure non est recedendum.*[75] The novel opinions proposed in recent years constitute a danger to the ecclesiastical discipline, and at the same time take care of but a few, extraordinary circumstances that the traditional interpretation does not embrace. The law-maker is not presumed to legislate for every possible contingency; he cares only for the general welfare. If these few, rare cases are not provided for by the law, the loss of souls does not necessarily follow. The following pious, but solid, reflections will bear this out:

1. The Sacraments are the usual, not the exclusive channels of grace. God, Who knows the hearts of men, can provide in the unusual way for the unusual case.[76]

2. Penitents frequently make acts of perfect contrition, or are already in the state of grace.

3. The Sacrament of Extreme Unction remits sin.[77]

4. The Sacraments of the living confer *gratiam primam* to those who approach them in good faith with attrition; penitents, however, usually approach the Eucharistic Table at the first opportunity.

These facts, not forgotten by the legislator, go to show that

---

[73] *Summula Theologiae Moralis,* III, n. 328, not. 50.

[74] *De Justitia et Jure,* D. 37, n. 26.

[75] Can. 6, n. 4.

[76] Cf. Reiffenstuel, lib. III, tit. XLIII, n. 3.

[77] James, V, 15.

although the Church does not supply jurisdiction as lavishly as some writers would desire, she is ever the *pia Mater Ecclesia.*[78]

ARTICLE II—JURISDICTION SUPPLIED IN DOUBT

Doubt, accepted in the subjective sense, is that state of mind in which the intellect suspends judgment between two or more opposed propositions; the intellect cannot assent to one or other without fear of erring. If the mind assents to one of these propositions with prudent fear that the contrary might be true, such a state is called *opinion.* This, too, in a broad sense may be regarded as doubt.[79]

Doubt is *positive,* if there are serious motives for assenting to two or more of the opposed propositions; it is *negative,* if the entire reason for doubt consists in the absence of motives capable of provoking prudent assent.[80] Positive doubt is always *probable* doubt, since the motives on either side are serious ones.[81]

Doubt of law (*dubium iuris*) is verified when there is doubt concerning the existence or extent of a law. Doubt of fact (*dubium facti*) is present when it is question whether or not a particular fact or circumstance is verified.

By virtue of Canon 209 the Church will supply jurisdiction of either the internal or external forum in *positive and probable doubt either of law or of fact.* This provision is to afford clerics an authorized reflex principle by which practical certitude can be attained, when they are confronted by a difficulty arising from the interpretation of law; and at the same time to make remote the possibility of anxiety and scruples when in the exercise of their ministry a doubt of fact presents itself. Thus, it is doubtful whether the error of many or the error of a majority of the community constitutes common error; if the minister acts on the hypothesis that the error of many suffices, the Church will supply jurisdiction, even though such error is not in itself sufficient. This is doubt of law. Again, a priest

---

78 Grosam, "Der Beichtvater ohne Jurisdiction," *LQS,* LXXXII (1929), 120-4.

79 Aertnys-Damen, *Theologia Moralis,* I, n. 63.

80 Waffelaert, *De Dubio Solvendo in Re Morali,* n. 113.

81 Cappello, *De Sacramentis,* II, n. 497.

has good reason to believe that many of the community regard him as a competent confessor, though he is not certain of this fact; this is a doubt of fact and the Church will supply by reason of this doubt. If, however, a priest doubts whether or not his jurisdiction expires today or tomorrow, and he has no serious reason to assent to either proposition, he is in negative doubt and the Church will not supply.

Before the Code doubt of law gave rise to the term, *probable jurisdiction,* while doubt of fact was called *doubtful jurisdiction.* It was generally admitted that the Church supplied in the first instance, owing to a universal custom and to the acknowledged verification of common error caused by the controversies of the authors on matters of law.[82] On the other hand, it was the common teaching that the Church would not supply in doubt of fact.[83] This controversy has been ended by a favorable disposition of the Code; the Church supplies in all positive doubt.

Article III—The Licit Use of Supplied Jurisdiction

It is generally admitted that a grave reason is required in order that a priest make use of supplied jurisdiction in common error. In this case, conscious of the defect, he compels the Church to supply jurisdiction and thus avoids the usual methods prescribed by law for the acquisition of the same. The grave necessity of a penitent, the fear of grave scandal, or the multitude of penitents who desire to approach the altar on a feast, and who cannot be heard by the number of approved confessors available, seem to be sufficient causes, if common error is present.[84]

Less serious reason is required for the use of supplied jurisdiction in cases of doubt, since this provision is precisely for the purpose of tranquillizing the minister. Hence, in positive

---

[82] Lehmkuhl, *Theologia Moralis,* II, n. 388 ss; St. Alphonsus, VI, n. 573; Grassi, *Universa Theologia Moralis,* III, 240; Ballerini-Palmieri, *Opus Theologicum Morale,* V, 629.

[83] D'Annibale, *Summula Theologiae Moralis,* I, n. 80; Lehmkuhl, *op. cit.,* II, n. 389; Sasserath, *Cursus Theologiae Moralis,* IV, n. 120.

[84] Marc-Raus, *Institutiones Morales Alphonsianae,* II, n. 1761; Aertnys-Damen, *Theologia Moralis,* II, n. 360; cf. Raus, "Mangelnde Jurisdiktion und error communis," *LQS,* LXXV (1922), 297 ss.

doubt no grave reason is required, and a sufficient reason will almost always be present.[85]

In negative doubt a grave reason is required, and sacramental jurisdiction must then be exercised conditionally, for the Church does not supply. Hence, the act will only be valid if jurisdiction is actually enjoyed by the agent, independently of the principle of Canon 209.

[85] Noldin, *Summa Theologiae Moralis,* III, n. 346; Cappello, *De Sacramentis,* II, n. 500.

BIBLIOGRAPHY

SOURCES

Acta Apostolicae Sedis (*AAS*), Romae, 1909.
Acta Sanctae Sedis (*ASS*), 41 vols., Romae, 1865-1908.
Acta et Decreta Concilii Plenarii Baltimorensis III, Baltimorae, 1886.
Canones et Decreta Concilii Tridentini, 19 ed., Taurini, 1913.
Codex Iuris Canonici Pii X Pontificis Maximi iussu digestus, Benedicti Papae XV auctoritate promulgatus, Romae, 1918.
Codicis Iuris Canonici Fontes, 4 vols., Romae, 1923-1926.
Collectanea Sacrae Congregationis de Propaganda Fide (*Coll.*), 2 vols., Romae, 1907.
Corpus Iuris Canonici, ed. Richter-Friedberg, 2 vols., Lipsiae, 1922.
Corpus Iuris Civilis, ed. P. Drueger, Berolini, 1922.
Mansi, Joannes, *Sacrorum Conciliorum Nova et Amplissima Collectio*, 51 vols., Parisiis, 1902-19.
Thesaurus Resolutionum Sacrae Congregationis Concilii, 167 vols., Romae, 1718-1908.

WORKS OF REFERENCE

Adam, Alex., *Roman Antiquities*, New York, 1842.
Aertnys-Damen, *Theologia Moralis*, 11 ed., 2 vols., Taurini, 1928.
Alphonsus de Liguori, *Theologia Moralis*, 2 vols., Turoni, 1879.
Antoine, Paul Gabriel, *Theologia Moralis Universa*, ed. novissima, 6 vols., Avenione, 1818.
Arquer, Miguel de, *El Error Común y la Jurisdicción Eclesiastica*, 2 ed., Barcelona, 1927.
Augustine, Charles, *A Commentary on the New Code of Canon Law*, 8 vols., St. Louis, 1918-1922.
Ayrinhac, H. A., *General Legislation in the New Code of Canon Law*, New York, 1923.
———, *Marriage Legislation in the New Code of Canon Law*, New York, 1919.
———, *Penal Legislation in the New Code of Canon Law*, New York, 1920.
Badii, Caesar, *Institutiones Iuris Canonici*, 2 vols., Florentiae, 1921.
Bargilliat, M., *Praelectiones Iuris Canonici*, 2 vols., Paris, 1915.
Ballerini-Palmieri, *Opus Theologicum Morale*, 7 vols., Prati, 1893.
Benedictus XIV, *De Synodo Dioecesana*, 2 vols., Romae, 1806.
———, *Casus Conscientiae de mandato. . . . D. N. Papae Benedicti XIV propositi ac resoluti*, 5 vols., Monasterii, 1856.
Bernardinus a Piconio, *Epistolarum B. Pauli Apostoli Triplex Expositio*, 3 vols., Parisiis, 1869.
Biederlack-Führich, *De Religiosis*, Oeniponte, 1919.
Billuart, *Summa S. Thomae Hodiernis Academiarum Moribus Accommodata*, 8 vols., Paris.

Blat, Albertus, *Commentarium Textus Codicis Iuris Canonici,* 5 vols., Romae, 1921-1927.

Bouix, D., *De Judiciis Ecclesiasticis,* 3 ed., 2 vols., Parisiis, 1883.

Bouuaert-Simenon, *Manuale Iuris Canonici,* 2 ed., Bandae et Leodii, 1926.

Bucceroni, Ianuarius, *Casus Conscientiae,* 6 ed., 2 vols., Romae, 1918.

Buckland, W. W., *A Text-Book of Roman Law,* Cambridge, 1921.

———, *A Manual of Roman Private Law,* Cambridge, 1925.

Busenbaum, H., *Medulla Theologiae Moralis,* Venetiis, 1698.

Cappello, Felix, *Tractatus Canonico-Moralis de Censuris,* 2 ed., Taurinorum Augustae, 1925.

———, *Tractatus Canonico-Moralis de Sacramentis,* 2 ed., 3 vols., Taurinorum Augustae, 1926-1928.

———, *Summa Iuris Publici Ecclesiastici,* Romae, 1923.

Cerato, Prosdocimus, *Matrimonium a Codice Iuris Canonici Desumptum,* 4 ed., Patavii, 1927.

Chelodi, Joannes, *Ius de Personis,* Tridenti, 1922.

———, *Ius Matrimonalie,* 3 ed., Tridenti, 1921.

Chokier, Erasmus, *Tractatus de Iurisdictione Ordinarii in Exemptos,* Coloniae-Agrippinae, 1629.

Cicognani, Hamletus, *Commentarium ad Librum I Codicis,* Romae, 1925.

Cimetier, F., *Pour étudier le Code de Droit Canonique,* Paris, 1927.

Cornelius a Lapide, *Commentaria in Omnes D. Pauli Epistolas,* 2 ed., Venetiis, 1717.

Cocchi, Guidus, *Commentarium in Codicem Iuris Canonici,* 7 vols., Taurionorum-Augustae, 1925.

D'Annibale, Josephus, *Summula Theologiae Moralis,* 2 ed., Mediolani, 1881.

DeAngelis, Philippus, *Praelectiones Iuris Canonici,* Romae, 1877.

Declareuil, J., *Rome the Law-Giver,* London-New York, 1927.

DeLugo, Joannes, *Disputationes Scholasticae et Morales,* 8 vols., Paris, 1868-1869.

DeMeester, A., *Iuris Canonici et Iuris Canonico-Civilis Compendium,* 3 vols., Brugis, 1921-1928.

DeSmet, Aloysius, *Tractatus Theologico-Canonicus de Sponsalibus et Matrimonio,* 4 ed., Brugis, 1927.

DeRosa, *De Executoribus Litterarum Apostolicarum,* Aschaffenburci, 1747.

Devoti, Joannes, *Institutionum Canonicarum Libri IV,* Leodii, 1883.

———, *Jus Canonicum Universum Publicum et Privatum,* 3 vols., Romae, 1837.

Duchesne, Louis, *Early History of the Christian Church,* translated from the French, 2 vols., New York, 1909-1912.

Fagnanus, Prosperus, *Commentarium in Libros Decretalium,* Venetiis, 1729.

Fanfani, P. Ludovicus, *De Iure Parochorum,* Turin, 1924.

———, *Il Diritto delle Religiose,* Turin, 1922.

Farrugia, Nicolaus, *De Matrimonio et Causis Matrimonialibus,* Taurini-Romae, 1924.

Febronius, Justin, *De Statu Ecclesiae et Legitima Potestate Romani Pontificis Liber Singularis ad Reuniendos Dissidentes in Religione Christianos Compositus,* Bullioni, 1764.

Ferraris, Lucius, *Prompta Bibliotheca Canonica,* 9 vols., Romae, 1885-1892.

Ferreres, Joannes, *Compendium Theologiae Moralis ad Norman Codicis Iuris Canonici,* 6 ed., 3 vols., Barcinone, 1925.

———, *Casus Conscientiae,* 5 ed., 2 vols., Barcinone, 1926.

Forti, Pierre, *De Judice Conservatore Regularium,* Mutinae, 1743.
Funk, F. X., *A Manual of Church History,* transl., 2 vols., St. Louis, 1921.
Gasparri, Petrus, *Tractatus Canonicus de Matrimonio,* 2 ed., 2 vols., Paris, 1892.
———, *Tractatus Canonicus de Sacra Ordinatione,* 2 vols., Paris, 1893.
Gennari, Casmirus, *Consultationes de Morale,* Paris, 1907-1910.
Golden, *Parochial Benefices in the New Code,* Washington, 1921.
Gossuet, *Théologie Morale a l'usage des Curés et des Confesseurs,* 10 ed., 2 vols., Paris, 1855.
Grassi, *Universa Theologia Moralis,* 3 vols., Aesii, 1854.
Gury-Ballerini, *Compendium Theologiae Moralis,* 10 ed., 2 vols., Romae, 1889.
Hardouin, *Conciliorum Collectio Regia Maxima,* 12 vols., Paris, 1715.
Hefele-Clarke, *A History of the Christian Councils,* transl., 2 vols., Edinburgh, 1876-1883.
Hinchius, P., *System des Katholischen Kirchenrechts,* 4 vols., Berlin, 1888.
Hyland, Francis, *Excommunication, Its Nature, Historical Development and Effects,* Washington, 1928.
Kelly, James, *The Jurisdiction of the Confessor,* New York, 1929.
Laymann, Paul, *Theologia Moralis,* 5 vols., Lutetiae Parisiorum, 1627.
Leage, R. W., *Roman Private Law,* London, 1924.
Lega, Michael, *Compendium Praelectionum de Judiciis Ecclesiasticis,* Romae, 1906.
Lehmkuhl, Augustinus, *Theologia Moralis,* 3 ed., 2 vols., Friburgi Brisgoviae, 1886.
MacEvilly, *An Exposition of the Epistles of St. Paul and of the Catholic Epistles,* 2 vols., Dublin, 1875.
Mackenzie, *Studies in Roman Law,* Edinburgh, 1862.
Marc-Gestermann-Raus, *Institutiones Morales Alphonsianae,* 18 ed., 2 vols., Lugduni, 1928.
Maroto, Philippus, *Institutiones Iuris Canonici,* 3 ed., 2 vols., Romae, 1921.
McGiffert, Arthur Cushman, *A History of Christianity in the Apostolic Age,* New York, 1900.
Menochio, Jacobus, *De Praesumptionibus, Conjecturis, Signis et Indiciis Commentaria,* 2 vols., Colonia Allobrogum, 1684.
Migne, *Patrologia Graeca,* 161 vols., Paris, 1858-1864.
———, *Patrologia Latina,* 221 vols., Paris, 1847-1870.
———, *Scripturae Sacrae Cursus Completus,* 28 vols, Paris, 1862.
Moran, *The Government of the Church in the First Century,* Maynooth, 1913.
Morey, William, *Outlines of Roman Law,* 2 ed., New York, 1914.
Motry, Hubert, *Diocesan Faculties according to the Code of Canon Law,* Washington, 1922.
Noldin, H., *Summa Theologiae Moralis,* 3 vols, Oeniponte, 1923-1924.
Noval, Josephus,*De Judiciis,* Augustae Taurinorum, 1920.
Ojetti, Benedictus, *Commentarium in Codicem Iuris Canonici,* Romae, 1927
O'Keeffe, Gerald, *Matrimonial Dispensations, Powers of Bishops, Priests and Confessors,* Washington, 1927.
Pallotini, Salvator, *Collectio Omnium Conclusionum et Resolutionum quae in causis propositis apud S. Congregationem Cardinalium S. Concilii Tridentini Interpretum prodierunt,* Romae, 1887.

Pesch, Christianus, *Praelectiones Dogmaticae,* 9 vols., Friburgi Brisgoviae, 1920.

Phillips, Georgius, *Compendium Iuris Ecclesiastici,* 1 ed., Latina, Ratisbonae, 1875.

Pius VI, *Responsio ad Metropolitanos super Nunciaturis Apostolicis,* Romae, 1789.

Pihring, *Jus Canonicum in V Libros Decretalium,* Dilingae, 1674.

Poste, Edward, *Gai Institutiones or Institutes of Roman Law by Gajus,* 4 ed., Oxford, 1904.

Prümmer, Dominicus, *Manuale Iuris Canonici,* 3 ed., Friburgi Brisgoviae, 1922.

Prateio, P., *Lexicon Iuris Civilis et Canonici,* Lugduni, 1567.

Radin, Max, *Handbook of Roman Law,* St. Paul, 1927.

Raus, J. B., *De Sacrae Obedientiae Virtute et Voto,* Lugduni, 1923.

Reiffenstuel, Anacletus, *Jus Canonicum Universum,* 4 vols., Venice, 1735.

Richter, *Canones et Decreta Concilii Tridentini,* Lipsiae, 1853.

Roberti, Franciscus, *De Processibus,* Romae, 1926.

Ruffini, Ernest, *Introductio in Novum Testamentum,* 2 vols., Romae, 1927.

Ryan, James H., *An Introduction to Philosophy,* New York, 1924.

Sanchez, Thomas, *De Sancto Matrimonii Sacramento,* Antverpiae, 1626.

Santi, Franciscus, *Praelectiones Iuris Canonici,* 2 vols., Ratisbon, 1892.

Sasserath, *Cursus Theologiae Moralis,* 6 ed., Augustae Vindelicorum, 1787.

Scavini, *Theologia Moralis Universa,* 11 ed., 3 vols., Mediolani, 1869.

Schäfer, Timotheus, *De Religiosis,* Münster, 1927.

Schmalzgrueber, Franciscus, *Jus Ecclesiasticum Universum,* 12 vols., Romae, 1843-1845.

Sherman, *Roman Law in the Modern World,* 2 ed., 3 vols., New York, 1924.

Suarez, Franciscus, *Opera Omnia,* 26 vols., Paris, 1861.

Tanquerey, Ad., *Brevior Synopsis Theologiae Dogmaticae,* 5 ed., Paris, 1923.

Theodoretus, *B. Theodoreti Episcopi Cyrensis Ecclesiasticae Historiae Libri Quinque,* Halae, 1770.

Thomas Aquinas, *Commentaria in Omnes D. Pauli Apostoli Epistolas,* 3 vols., Paris, 1874.

———, *Summa Theologica,* Taurini, 1917.

Thomassinus, Ludovicus, *Vetus et Nova Ecclesiae Disciplinae,* Mogontiaci, 1787.

Van Espen, Z. B., *Jus Ecclesiasticum Universum,* Venetiis, 1769.

Van Steenkiste, *S. Pauli Epistolae Breviter Explicatae,* 3 ed., 2 vols., Brugis, 1876.

Vermeersch, Arthurus, *Theologiae Moralis Principia, Responsa, Consilia,* 2 ed., 4 vols., Romae, 1926-1928.

Vermeersch-Creusen, *Epitome Iuris Canonici,* 3 ed., 3 vols., Mechlinae-Romae, I, II (1927), III (1928).

Vlaming, Th. M., *Praelectiones Iuris Matrimonii,* 3 ed., 2 vols., Bussum, 1919-1921.

Waffelaert, G. J., *De Dubio Solvendo in re Morali,* Lovanii, 1880.

Walsh, Gulielmus, *Tractatus de Actibus Humanis,* Dublin, 1880.

Wernz, Franciscus, *Jus Decretalium,* 3 ed., 8 vols., Prati, 1913.

Wernz-Vidal, *Jus Canonicum,* 3 vols., Romae, 1923-1927.

Woywood, Stanislaus, *A Practical Commentary on the Code of Canon Law,* 2 vols., New York, 1925.

Zaplotnik, Joannes, *De Vicariis Foraneis,* Washington, 1927.

PERIODICALS

American Ecclesiastical Review (*AER*), Philadelphia, 1889—
Apollinaris, Romae, 1928—
Archiv fur katholisches Kirchenrecht (*AkKR*), Mainz, 1857—
Canoniste Contemporain, Le, Paris, 1878—
Homiletic and Pastoral Review, New York, 1900—
Il Monitore Ecclesiastico, Romae, 1888—
Irish Ecclesiastical Record, Dublin, 1897—
Jus Pontificium Juridica Ephemeris, Romae, 1921—
Linzer Theologisch-Praktische Quartalschrift, Linz, 1832—
Nouvelle Revue Theologique, Paris, 1856—
Perfice Munus, Torino, 1926—
Razon y Fe, Madrid, 1901—

Universitas Catholica Americae

WASHINGTON, D. C.

FACULTAS IURIS CANONICI

1929

No. 55

DEUS LUX MEA

THESES

QUAS

AD DOCTORATUS GRADUM

IN

IURECANONICO

APUD UNIVERSITATEM CATHOLICAM AMERICAE

CONSEQUENDUM

PUBLICE PROPUGNABIT

RAYMUNDUS AUGUSTINUS KEARNEY

SACERDOS DIOECESIS BROOKLYNIENSIS

SACRAE THEOLOGIAE DOCTOR

ET

IURIS CANONICI LICENTIATUS

HORA IX A. M. DIE XXVIII MAII A. D. MCMXXIX

TITULI

DE IURE CANONICO

I.	De Dissertatione.	
II.	De Historia Iuris Canonici.	
III.	De Ratione inter Ecclesiam et Statum.	
IV.	Canones 1–7	De Ambitu Codicis.
V.	Canones 8–24	De Legibus Ecclesiasticis.
VI.	Canones 25–30	De Consuetudine.
VII.	Canones 31–35	De Temporis Supputatione.
VIII.	Canones 36–62	De Rescriptis.
IX.	Canones 63–79	De Privilegiis.
X.	Canones 80–86	De Dispensationibus.
XI.	Canones 356–362	De Synodo Dioecesana.
XII.	Canones 363–390	De Curia Dioecesana.
XIII.	Canones 423–428	De Consultoribus Dioecesanis.
XIV.	Canones 451–478	De Parochis et Vicariis Paroecialibus.
XV.	Canones 479–486	De Ecclesiarum Rectoribus.
XVI.	Canones 487–498	De Notione Religionis, et de Erectione et Suppressione Religionis, Provinciae, Domus.
XVII.	Canones 499–537	De Religionum Regimine.
XVIII.	Canones 538–586	De Admissione in Religionem.
XIX.	Canones 587–591	De Ratione Studiorum in Religionibus Clericalibus.
XX.	Canones 592–631	De Obligationibus et Privilegiis Religiosorum.
XXI.	Canones 632–672	De Transitu ad Aliam Religionem, de Egressu e Religione, et de Dimissione Religiosorum.
XXII.	Canones 673–681	De Societatibus in Communi Viventium Sine Votis.
XXIII.	Canones 726–730	De Simonia.
XXIV.	Canones 951–991	De Ministro et Subjecto Sacrae Ordinationis.
XXV.	Canones 1094–1103	De Forma Celebrationis Matrimonii.
XXVI.	Canones 1104–1109	De Matrimonio Conscientiae et de Tempore et Loco Celebrationis Matrimonii.
XXVII.	Canones 1110–1117	De Matrimonii Effectibus.
XXVIII.	Canones 1118–1141	De Separatione Coniugum et de Matrimonii Convalidatione.
XXIX.	Canones 1552–1568	De Notione Iudicii et de Foro Competenti.

XXX.	Canones 1569–1607	De Variis Tribunalium Gradibus et Speciebus.
XXXI.	Canones 1608–1645	De Disciplina in Tribunalibus Servanda.
XXXII.	Canones 1646–1666	De Partibus in Causa.
XXXIII.	Canones 1667–1705	De Actionibus et Exceptionibus.
XXXIV.	Canones 1706–1725	De Causae Introductione.
XXXV.	Canones 1726–1731	De Litis Contestatione.
XXXVI.	Canones 1742–1746	De Interrogationibus Partibus in Iudicio Faciendis.
XXXVII.	Canones 1960–1992	De Causis Matrimonialibus.
XXXVIII.	Canones 1993–1998	De Causis Contra Sacram Ordinationem.
XXXIX.	Canones 2195–2198	De Natura Delicti Eiusque Divisione.
XL.	Canones 2199–2211	De Imputabilitate Delicti, de Causis Aggravantibus vel Minuentibus, et de Iuridicis Delicti Effectibus.
XLI.	Canones 2212–2213	De Conatu Delicti.
XLII.	Canones 2214–2240	De Poenis in Genere.
XLIII.	Canones 2241–2285	De Poenis Medicinalibus seu de Censuris.
XLIV.	Canones 2286–2305	De Poenis Vindicativis.
XLV.	Canones 2306–1213	De Remediis Poenalibus et Poenitentiis.

DE IURE ROMANO

XLVI. The periods of Roman Law.
XLVII. Personality.
XLVIII. Slavery.
XLIX. Citizenship.
L. The Roman family.
LI. Exheredatio.
LII. Praeteritio.
LIII. Omissio.
LIV. Classes of Heirs.
LV. Institution and substitution of heirs.
LVI. Legacies.
LVII. Fideicommissa.
LVIII. Intestate succession.
LIX. General principles of obligation.
LX. Contracts.

Vidit Facultas:

PHILIPPUS BERNARDINI, S.T.D., J.U.D., Decanus.
LUDOVICUS H. MOTRY, S.T.D., J.C.D., a Secretis.
VALENTINUS T. SCHAAF, O.F.M., J.C.D.
FRANCISCUS J. LARDONE, S.T.D., J.U.D.

Vidit Rector Magnificus Universitatis:

JACOBUS HUGO RYAN, Ph.D., S.T.D.

BIOGRAPHICAL NOTE

Raymond A. Kearney was born on September 25, 1902. He received his elementary education at Nativity Academy in the diocese of Brooklyn, N. Y. He then attended Brooklyn Preparatory School, and in 1923 received the degree of Bachelor of Arts from Holy Cross College, Worcester, Mass. He prepared for the priesthood at the North American College, Rome, Italy, and was ordained on March 12, 1927. He attained the degree of Doctor in Sacred Theology at the University of the Propaganda in 1927. In the same year he entered the School of Canon law of the Catholic University of America, and in 1928 was awarded the degree of Licentiate in Canon Law.

www.ingramcontent.com/pod-product-compliance
Lightning Source LLC
LaVergne TN
LVHW050220080826
844660LV00012B/441
* 9 7 8 0 8 1 3 2 2 2 4 4 8 *